Praise for Headstrong Performance

Ron Kaufman, New York Times bestselling author of "Uplifting Service" says:

> *"Marcel has written a breakthrough book connecting the insights of neuroscience with the reality of our daily lives. These ideas and exercises deliver immediate performance improvements in your health, your happiness and your success in life. Read this book today to perform better tomorrow."*

Dr. Roy Sugarman, Neuropsychologist and author of "Saving Your Life One Day at a Time: Seven Ways to Survive the Modern World" and "Client-Centered Training: A Trainer and Coach's Guide to Motivating Clients" says:

> *"Having met Marcel, you will immediately observe his passion, professionalism and commitment to his cause, namely, helping others do things just a little bit better every day, and become therefore a better person, every day of their lives. This commitment comes out clearly in his writing, and I recommend his new book with enthusiasm."*

Colin Sampson, Senior Vice President, SAP says:

> *"Headstrong Performance is a life-changing message about healthy work-life balance, good nutrition, rest and regular exercise, all leading to an improvement in performance, individually and as a team. A great way to bring about real, positive and productive change."*

MARCEL DAANE

HEADSTRONG PERFORMANCE

IMPROVE YOUR MENTAL PERFORMANCE WITH NUTRITION, EXERCISE, AND NEUROSCIENCE

Headstrong Performance
© 2015 Marcel Daane

ISBN Hardcover : 978-981-09-3097-4
ISBN Paperback : 978-981-09-3098-1
ISBN Digitized   : 978-981-09-3100-1
ISBN E-Book   : 978-981-09-3099-8

First print edition: January 2015

Published by:
B.B.P.C. Singapore

Table of Contents

Acknowledgements

First and foremost, I would like to say thanks to my mother and father for raising me with a strong set of core, consistent values that have functioned as a guiding light through my very colorful life, even during times of perceived darkness.

To my beautiful wife, Ursula, who patiently stood by me during the many months of writing this book and during my preceding years of research. I will always be grateful for your love and support.

To my amazing daughter, Kilani. You have been the greatest gift I could ever have asked for. Without you, I would not be where I am today.

Further, I would like to say thank you to everyone who inspired me to remain headstrong in my personal fitness pursuits as well as through my academic journey over the years, which ultimately enabled me to conceive the concept of "Headstrong Performance."

I am in your debt.

Thank you all.

Preface

Coming from a leadership consultant, using the word "headstrong" in the title of a book may seem a bit odd. By the standard definition, someone who is headstrong tends to be stubborn and immovable. These could possibly be interpreted as negative attributes in a leader. And the rigid, authoritative leader of yesteryear has long been proven to lack effectiveness compared to the modern-day transformational leader who specializes in the art of interpersonal communications.

In my years pursuing post-graduate qualifications in Neuroscience and Leadership, I was exposed to a multitude of leadership models and leadership research that spanned more than a century. Along with the academic knowledge I acquired, I also had the privilege of working with highly effective leaders through my own research and work conducted in collaboration with organizations such as The Center for Creative Leadership, or CCL.

My research and work covered multiple arenas from the military to Fortune 500 companies, to service industries and education. This exposure and experience opened my eyes to what is really required from a great leader. This in turn inspired me to not only be a better leader but a better person, husband and father.

Through my own life's journey as well as these leadership experiences, I began to notice that while being headstrong might not be appropriate in some leadership contexts, aspects of it seem essential for success in others. There are numerous examples throughout history where monumental and world-altering milestones were achieved because people remained headstrong – firm and unwavering – in their core values and self-belief.

Consider the persistent Thomas Edison inventing the light bulb, or Nelson Mandela and Mahatma Gandhi defying suppressive political regimes. And there are scores of other modern-day individuals who defied all odds because they never quit believing in themselves or their purpose, and were determined to emerge victorious.

The title *Headstrong Performance* in this context therefore implies a level of motivation and unyielding dedication to be the best we can be, whatever we do.

My unique background blending nutrition, exercise and neuroscience complements my research in leadership, and has enabled me to develop a holistic perspective on how we can get the most out of our performance and our lives.

For that reason, I developed a number of performance strategies that are designed to fuel the brain and develop capacity for improved performance. At a foundational level, you may be familiar with many of these brain-capacity-generating strategies. But putting them into context, as part of a dedicated plan to improve mental *and* physical performance, offers a fresh perspective with literally life-altering consequences.

These strategies are the culmination of decades of work and research. They are practical strategies that I still employ in my coaching practice today.

I hope you're entertained and engaged by the contents of this book, but even more importantly, I hope that you put into action some of the suggestions that I present here. The positive effects may surprise you.

My warmest and best wishes to you,

How To Read This Book

This book is dedicated to everyone who has struggled or is currently struggling with finding balance in their lives, between their own health and the sacrifices they need to make to stay ahead of the game.

For those who believe that to even consider adding some health behaviors into our daily regimens is simply too difficult, too time-consuming, or even irrelevant to human performance – this book is designed to show you why health is intricately linked to performance. And further, this book offers a number of practical, easy-to-implement strategies that can be incorporated into the busiest of lifestyles.

Integrating neuroscience, exercise and nutrition creates an extremely powerful approach to enhancing performance. Of course, they're also diverse and sometimes technical topics, so one of my major challenges here has been to present scientific data in an enjoyable and easy-to-comprehend manner, without sacrificing scientific integrity.

To achieve this, *Headstrong Performance* is divided into four main topic sections: **Stress and Resilience, Optimizing Sustained Attention, Boosting Creativity and Insight,** and **Creating Change**.

Each of these sections starts with a chapter on the science behind the topic at hand, followed by a chapter focusing on strategies to apply that science, and finishing with a case study that puts the science and strategies into context.

For some of you, the scientific chapters may seem a bit challenging at times, but I encourage you to bear with them and take your time absorbing the information. The scientific chapters add depth and context to the strategies, and will help you understand many of the scientific underpinnings of our behavior under pressure.

The third chapter in each section will connect the dots between the science and day-to-day behavior as you read the case study. You'll get a real-world sense of how these strategies can be implemented, and the impact they can have.

Chapters 1 and 2 of this book introduce the concept of Headstrong Performance as it relates to my own past experience as well as four years of research on the topic.

Chapters 3, 4 and 5 focus on stress and resilience. Chapter 3 explains the neuroscientific underpinnings of stress and resilience, Chapter 4 offers practical strategies for managing stress and improving resilience, and Chapter 5 adds context with a case study from my daily work as a coach.

Chapters 6, 7 and 8 follow suit. Chapter 6 delves into the neuroscience behind sustained attention, Chapter 7 shares strategies to optimize sustained attention, and Chapter 8 makes the practice of these strategies real with another case study.

Chapters 9, 10 and 11 focus on the science behind creativity and insight, followed by strategies and another case study.

Chapters 12, 13 and 14 follow the same format with a look at the science behind changing behavior, followed by strategies for change and a final case study.

In **Chapter 15**, we will explore how to integrate the strategies from the previous chapters into an achievable action plan.

My goal for everyone reading this book is the same as for every one of my clients and workshop participants. I hope that each person will walk away inspired to introduce healthy behaviors into their lifestyles, and discover that health not only improves individual or organizational performance, but can positively change their lives and the lives of their loved ones in the process.

I hope this book will do the same for you.

Chapter One

Perspective

"The mark of the immature man is that he wants to die nobly for a cause, while the mark of a mature man is that he wants to live humbly for one."

Wilhelm Stekel

As we get started on this journey together, I would like to take a moment to explain to you why this is such an important book for me.

I don't come from a typical corporate background. I don't have a fancy leadership title. I'm not an award-winning author, nor do I aspire to be one. I'm not a CEO of a large Fortune 500 company. In fact, I might be exactly the opposite of what one might expect from the author of a leadership-type book. It's for that reason entirely that I am writing this book about leadership and performance.

What you'll find out in the next few paragraphs is that I come from a unique background – one that I believe will allow me to provide you with a completely different perspective on leadership and performance. In turn, this will add value to your existing skill set as an executive and leader.

My experiences, combined with academic knowledge on leadership and my research as a neuroleadership researcher, have taught me that in order for us to be able to change, we need to be able to see different perspectives. For that to happen, we need to be willing to broaden our scope of perspective and expand our minds beyond the realm of our perceived limitations. My intention is that this book will help you broaden your perspective and tap into areas of consciousness that you may not have considered – helping you become a more effective leader in any capacity where you serve.

The fact that I come from an unconventional background isn't meant as an apology or a mere autobiographical detail. I believe that leaders need to spurn convention and be able to switch to a different perspective – by doing so themselves and by encouraging others to do it.

To the world, I'm sure my childhood looked quite normal. However, behind closed doors, my household was very different. I grew up in a typical suburban neighborhood, much like many other kids. I played outside with my friends and went to a typical school. Like so many of my friends back then, my dad worked a typical day job and my mom was a stay-at-home mom who was often cooking, cleaning and doing laundry.

So when my friends came to visit, they never noticed anything different about my family or about my mom in particular. But besides being a devoted mother and housekeeper, my mother had another occupation that consumed much of her attention and energy.

My mom was a housekeeper by day, and a political activist by night. And the regime she fought against designated her a terrorist.

About 65 years ago, my mom – a Caucasian-born South African – was a little girl who found herself living under a white supremacist political regime we know as apartheid. She grew up witnessing many gruesome acts of cruelty toward native South Africans. Instead of complying with apartheid, like most white children, my mother developed a deep hatred for it and for any injustice perpetrated upon another human being. She became one of very few white South African women who publicly opposed apartheid.

One can only imagine how much trouble her strong sense of righteousness got her into, and the embarrassment she must have been to the white supremacist government. When I was a boy, my mother confided in me that she was eventually jailed for her public political activities, and finally, exiled from the country she loved so dearly. Thus, I was born in political exile in the Netherlands.

I had two brothers and one sister, and as children we spent much of our childhood witnessing our mom continuing to fight with amazing passion against this government. The unfair and racist treatment of her fellow South Africans ignited a rage within my mother that only became greater every day she was forced to live away from her motherland.

My mother's strong stance against apartheid gave her a tremendous sense of purpose that I have witnessed in only a few people in my life. She fought tirelessly for 50 years while living abroad in political exile. She sacrificed everything to make sure that she would always be a thorn in the side of the South African government. In the end, her headstrong persistence paid off. In 1994, the apartheid regime crumbled.

This taught me very early on that definitions are created from particular perspectives. The word "terrorist" is a *perspective* – not an objective, unassailable fact. To us, of course, my mom wasn't a terrorist in any sense. She was a freedom fighter, and one of the most courageous people I have ever known. She believed in freedom for all people. But in South Africa, opposing the fundamental values of the ruling elite made her a terrorist to that regime.

After the fall of the regime, my parents moved back to South Africa, and in 2009 my mother was awarded the prestigious Order of Luthuli award, which could be considered the South African equivalent of the British knighthood.

I learned two valuable lessons from my mom that have stuck with me throughout my life, and they've become the core values through which I live life and apply myself in my leadership practice.

My mom's first lesson: Never, ever surrender our integrity. Our integrity, my mom always used to say, is what determines our character. And no matter what happens in life, we must remain steadfast in our core values of fairness, courage and honesty, because they determine who we are at all times, in every situation. She taught me that life can strip us of everything we have in an instant, and the only things we may have left at the end of the day are our integrity and our character.

That impressed me enormously as a child. Through this lesson, I developed core values such as fairness, courage, honesty and standing up for the underdog (which of course was a very strong ethic in our household).

My mom's second lesson: Life has much greater meaning when we do things for others and not just for ourselves. That was a powerful lesson because my mom sacrificed everything we had. We did not grow up as wealthy people because my mom's life was mainly dedicated to being a freedom fighter, and there's not a lot of money in that line of work. It was a sacrifice she gladly made. And it's a sacrifice that we all as a family supported. Especially as young boys, it was pretty cool knowing our mom was a freedom fighter standing up for something much greater than herself. I can tell you it would have made a great topic during career day at school.

Naturally, however, life in political exile is not all rainbows and sunshine. There are also some downsides to having a freedom fighter as a mom. First of all, I grew up in an environment of anger. Even though the anger was not necessarily directed at me personally, I often perceived my mom as being extremely angry – because she was. She was always literally putting up a fight, and this was difficult for me to understand as a child. Even though I knew I was loved, that feeling was often overshadowed by the constant battles going on inside her and with the regime she opposed. This left me confused.

Secondly, I had great difficulty fitting in with other kids. While I was daily immersed in core values such as fairness, integrity and standing up for others, most of the other kids never gave much thought to these notions. Nor were they even exposed to the worldly problems that were part of our everyday lives. That created a disconnect between other kids and me.

I did have friends who I played with, but I was never able to connect with them at an emotional and worldly level. I often found myself in friendships that seemed shallow, without emotional substance. This resulted in a sense of isolation. I always had difficulty relating to kids who, in my opinion, did not see the big picture.

Moreover, living in an environment fueled by anger and hostility against an oppressive government, I grew up believing that I needed to emulate my mother by being a warrior. To many people, that might seem cool, but as a kid it made it much harder to fit into society. Not surprisingly, perhaps, I found happiness in the martial arts at a very young age. Being a warrior-minded kid, martial arts came naturally to me and I excelled in them.

After graduating from high school, I encountered my first serious life challenge, in which I found myself torn between my core values and society's norms. Like any other high school graduate, I had to decide what I wanted to do with my life. I had tremendous difficulty figuring out the right path for me. I was interested in health and medicine, but I didn't think my grades were good enough to get me into medical school. In retrospect, I was extremely troubled and did not have much self-confidence.

The military appeared to be a natural place for me because it seemed to represent my core values of integrity, fairness, courage, honesty and serving others over myself. So at a very young age, I joined the Dutch Royal Navy and served for 10 years. It was definitely an ideal environment for me in many ways. Serving my country for a decade affirmed my sense that there's much greater meaning in life by doing something for others than simply trying to satisfy myself.

Unfortunately, though, I also had a dark side, and that dark side started to come out in the Navy. While serving, I discovered there were two paths one can follow in this environment. One is the path of health, fitness and operational readiness, serving in a highly physical environment such as the Navy Seals. The other track involves monotonous, boring jobs that can lead to understimulation, which in turn can drive people to experiment with drugs and alcohol during their service.

I found myself operating in the latter environment, working in Naval Intelligence. Too many long nights reading situation reports and plotting Soviet movements caused my brain to start seeking excitement in the form of drugs and alcohol. In those days – we're talking the early 1980s – the Dutch Royal Navy was very accepting of alcohol outside of the workplace as long as it didn't interfere with work performance. For some reason, I managed to get away with some serious drinking outside of work because I could still function in my monotonous job. Eventually, I became chemically dependent on alcohol and abused recreational drugs on a very regular basis. In fact, I was a functioning alcoholic, until one day, I could not function at work without the occasional drink during work hours. That's when I got caught.

In most Navies, getting caught with liquor would probably lead to a dishonorable discharge. Because I was a first-time offender, however, I got lucky and escaped discharge or even severe penalty. Instead, I received orders to report to my new station in the Caribbean. Yes, the Dutch Navy actually sent me out to the Caribbean for a year, where I had the good fortune to train and operate with the Dutch Royal Marines as a member of their recon and anti-piracy division. In this training, I was required to be operationally ready 24 hours per day.

Working out for six to eight hours a day and having no access to alcohol or drugs literally transformed my life. It was the first time I had experienced how health and fitness can not only change someone's life, but can actually save it. After that year with the Marines, I left the Caribbean an entirely different person. I was a man transformed.

I was stationed back on board ships and inside bunkers, and again bored out of my mind. Knowing what this environment led to the first time around, I didn't feel comfortable there any longer. I knew I could offer more and do more with my life. I didn't know what, and I certainly didn't know how or even why. But I knew I had to leave. So in the early 1990s, I resigned from the Dutch Royal Navy and tried to make a go of it in civilian society.

Even though I no longer felt at home in the military, the transition from military to civilian life was extremely difficult for me. I had a hard time fitting in, or finding the type of job and corporate culture that would allow me to feel like I could live by my core values. I began by working in sales. And I tried really hard to be a successful salesman. I sold office equipment, which was beginning to boom in the 1990s. It worked all right initially, but after a while, I started feeling deeply unhappy. Going from office to office talking about fax machines and photocopiers was not satisfying. It simply didn't give me the sense of purpose that always burned bright in my soul.

The problem was, I didn't know what my purpose was *specifically*. I just knew that whenever I was in a situation that wasn't aligned with my values, I would feel miserable. For three years, I jumped from one sales job to another, never particularly successful and always feeling unfulfilled.

During my time in sales, I started to believe that maybe I was just a really bad salesperson. I've since learned that I'm actually a *good* salesperson. What I didn't know back then is that because I couldn't identify or connect emotionally with the *core values* of the sales companies who employed me, I had great difficulty staying engaged and connected with the jobs. I simply could not see how something like a fax machine could benefit somebody's life for the better. I therefore became disengaged and ended up moving on. And I'm sure that happens to many people in organizations today.

We now know, of course, that employee engagement and disengagement are enormous issues. They're key drivers of staff productivity and organizational performance. In the book "A Peacock in the Land of Penguins," the authors make the point that a corporate environment shapes employee expectations and behavior, often to a self-limiting degree. A culture can become a self-fulfilling prophecy.

Luckily, the Dutch unemployment system back then allowed me to take a one-year sabbatical with almost full pay because I had served in the Navy for at least 10 years. This law allowed me to resign from my job and take time off, during which I could learn a new trade. It was in that year that I was fortunate enough to discover what I was meant to do with my life.

I recall sitting at home and really giving some thought to what I wanted to do. What makes me happy? Throughout my entire life, the one thing that always made me happy was exercise. Exercise gave me great release and relief during my childhood, through the martial arts. Exercise also saved me in the Dutch Royal Navy. I wondered if exercise was an area in which I could work and make a contribution.

So I studied physical fitness, and by the time I was 29 I was certified as a personal trainer. The first gym that hired me in Holland was Gold's Gym. The wife of the owner was a physiotherapist and one day she asked me if I could work with one of her patients. This patient had been in a car accident. He was wheelchair-bound and immobile. At that point, doctors didn't know whether the spinal trauma would allow him to ever walk again.

Not being a physical therapist, I asked the owner's wife if she could teach me how I could best help this client. For days, she showed me exactly how to keep paralyzed limbs mobile with gentle stretching exercises, how to do core exercises while in a wheelchair, and the types of exercise the client needed to build his upper body strength.

With this newfound knowledge, I worked with the client following a program written by the physiotherapist. I patiently trained my client three times per week, working on his mobility, core stability and basically building his strength. After a few months, during one of our sessions together, I had one of the most profoundly emotional experiences I have ever had with a client.

I remember that moment vividly. After about one month, my client began to regain the feeling in his legs. During his physical therapy sessions at the hospital, he was able to walk with a great amount of support, but for the longest time, he did not feel strong enough to stand on his own. One day, after completing one of our sessions, he wanted to show me how much strength he had gained. He pushed himself off of his armrests and got up onto his feet and lifted himself up. I supported him and he held my hand and he got up on his feet and stood there.

For the first time since his accident, my client conjured up the courage to take his first few steps, and slowly started to shuffle forward while I supported him. I felt like the support I was giving him was so minimal that I decided to ease off and let him walk on his own as he kept shuffling forward. It wasn't until he had taken his first few steps that he realized I was no longer supporting him and he stopped dead in his tracks. We looked at each other for a little while and both started to cry.

For him, of course, the tears were wet, tangible evidence of the sheer happiness of being able to walk on his own, and to know that he was going to be okay. My tears and joy came from seeing somebody grow and become strong, and that I played an important part in his growth. It gave me goose bumps all over to know that I played a part in helping give this man his life back.

It was right then and there that I knew this was my purpose in life. I knew that I was put on this planet to help people improve their lives by being healthier and fitter. That experience put me on a path from which I have not deviated over the past 20 years.

The next major milestones in my life were meeting my wife, Ursula, and the birth of our daughter, Kilani. Even though I thought I was working with great purpose, it wasn't until I held my daughter in my arms for the very first time and looked into her eyes that I instantly knew that life was not just about me anymore. I was now responsible for making sure that somebody else was going to be okay. That intensified my purpose because it was at that exact moment that I also knew that I needed to do something constructive with my life. Not only to focus on dedicating my life to helping people, but at the same time to provide for my daughter, especially financially.

Initially, this was a source of great conflict for me, because it seemed that it was difficult to make money when you put the values of integrity, fairness and compassion above everything else. Just ask my mother. I felt increasingly challenged by the quest to find balance between my core values and materialism. But my daughter helped me focus that challenge in a constructive way. The day she was born, I knew I needed to be an even better person than I had been up to that point.

I went back to school and completed a degree in complementary medicine. This degree included courses in exercise therapy, movement therapy and applied nutrition. It was through applied nutrition and movement therapy that I started working with patients who suffered from all types of chronic illnesses and injuries.

During this period when I was working in the healthcare industry, my wife, who is a physical education teacher, said one day, "What we really need is a school that helps teach kids how to move. We need to provide children with a stronger foundation of confidence to be able to move, because they are growing up in a very sedentary world." As a physical education teacher, she was starting to see how a lot of kids were losing their ability to perform basic movements, such as the skills to sprint, stop, turn and jump with good technique. Kids from our generation learned these movements naturally through playing outside with friends. But many children these days are not learning these movements because they're growing up in controlled environments where physical play does not occur naturally.

My wife and I put together a business plan. Up to this point in my life I had not been involved in business except as an employee, and I had no idea what a business plan was, let alone how to write one. Nevertheless, we did it. It took me three months to write, but the plan attracted investors and allowed us to open a gym for kids called the Speed Institute.

Speed Institute was my real-world course in turning my expertise – the ability to help and teach people – into a business. It was through Speed Institute that I learned my first real lessons about leadership, and about how our decisions as leaders and business owners directly affect people at the ground level. A few years after Speed Institute was up and running successfully, I decided to take the opportunity to sell my shares in the business, and focus on adult education.

I went on to develop a scalable fitness coaching certification program that is now a global program, utilized by trainers, sports coaches and physical therapists. That system is called the MET (Move, Empower and Transform).

Because I had to make my skills scalable so other people could apply the teachings, I needed to inspire, motivate and instruct new trainers and coaches. This was a new challenge for someone who'd always been a solo practitioner.

While working with a team of people spread out around the world, I developed a whole new appreciation for management and leadership techniques. I realized my knowledge of effective leadership needed serious addressing if I wanted to ensure my team was performing consistently. It was through that process that I became fascinated with leadership.

As somewhat of a science geek with a degree in complementary medicine, I started exploring neuroscience and behavioral neuroscience, and I bumped into a university that runs a master's program in the Neuroscience of Leadership. I ended up completing a master's degree in the Neuroscience of Leadership from Middlesex University. This was one of the greatest learning experiences of my life, and a major game-changer for me not only as a leader, but also as a human being and a parent.

After I received my degree, I developed a new executive coaching and leadership development company called Headstrong Performance, which was inspired by four years of research during my master's program and is the inspiration for this book. Headstrong Performance uses a unique coaching model that integrates health, neuroscience and executive coaching.

Eventually, my success in leadership and fitness education gained the attention of Anytime Fitness, the world's largest gym franchise chain. In 2013, I was offered the role as Director of Organizational Performance for Anytime Fitness Asia, and I accepted. I conceptualized a brand-compliant learning and development model specifically for franchising. I learned early on that franchising is a unique business, as each outlet is privately owned.

Unlike traditional organizations where learning and development can easily be imposed onto departments and employees – franchise owners and their staff require intensive engagement strategies and incentives to not only attend training, but to want to apply what they learn in their outlets.

This experience provided me with fantastic opportunities to stretch my leadership and coaching abilities to the max, often with humbling results, as often things did not go as planned. Initially, progress was frustrating and slow, but persistence and patience paid off. Eventually, I managed to turn my academic leadership knowledge into an applicable model that was easily scalable and became one of the driving motors of Anytime Fitness Asia's success throughout the region. This experience enabled me to gain powerful insights about leadership and change, which in turn have added important fuel to this book and my practice as a Headstrong Performance Coach.

In retrospect, I have learned that our past experiences, even if they seem completely irrelevant, may help shape character, but they do not define who we will be in the future. That is determined by what we do with the *values* of the lessons learned from our past, and how we choose to use those values moving forward.

In my case, I learned that by being firm in my values, I was always able to find my way back to who I truly am – no matter how great my challenges, and no matter how clouded my vision may have been at times. Furthermore, exercise, health and fitness have been my guiding lights and have played a significant role in shaping me into the person I am today. In fact, time and again it has proven to be the *vehicle* for my values, my integrity and my commitment to helping others.

I hope that after reading this book, you too will see the importance of being headstrong in your values and your health behaviors. Whatever your challenges or distractions, this can help you improve your focus, creativity and performance at work and in life.

This book will also invite you to step outside the box and learn about different perspectives that might change the way you see the world – your world.

Skill can be taught, but values define character — which is the foundation of resilience, staying power and performance in all aspects of life.

Chapter Two

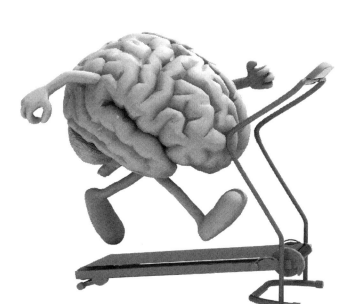

Health and Performance

Successful people realize the importance of a healthy body and a healthy mind. They know that the two are inextricably inter-linked and imperative for their smooth functioning."

Andy Paula

Six teenage volleyball players gathered around me just before they were about to play the game of the year in the National Championships. They had worked, trained and competed together for an entire year just to reach this point.

Outside of standard team practices, all of these girls spent countless additional hours refining their volleyball skills and improving their fitness on their own. They all sacrificed what other girls would consider fun time, such as time spent on social media, playing video games, staying up late during sleepovers and so on – with the hope that their sacrifices would help them make it to this point at the National Championships. Their dedication to the sport and to their team was inspirational, and I felt honored that my daughter wanted me to function as the team's performance coach.

Our ritual was to have a team conversation before and after each game, and this game was no exception. During the pre-game mental preparation, the girls sat around me in a circle and we talked about their expectations. They talked about how they wanted to win the game, which might be considered good enough motivation. But when I asked them *how* they planned to do that as a team, the girls went silent. As hard as they had prepared individually for the game, they had not considered preparing mentally as a team.

They had not given attention to how they were going to perform *together* for that game. There was an expectation to win – without a uniform agreement on what they would do, as a team, to achieve that. They were focused on the objective, but none of them had focused on the path that was going to take them there.

Research in sports psychology has shown that simply focusing on winning without focusing on *what* we're going to do, and *how well* we're going to do it, actually decreases performance success. With that in mind, I began to shift the conversation from the expectation to simply win the game, to focusing on playing as a uniform team and having loads of fun and laughter in the process. They performed mental drills together, imagining how they would pass the ball to each other and how they would work together to score the points needed for a win.

The girls walked onto the court as a unified team and totally nailed it that day – but it didn't happen without its challenges. During the first set of the game, one of the girls experienced a bit of a mental breakdown. She expected excellence from herself, but for some reason, her body seemed to stop doing what her mind wanted to do. Every ball she touched seemed to develop a life of its own and went in a completely different direction than planned.

During that time, her teammates had to support her by taking on the extra workload and expending greater energy to cover her. They also offered words of encouragement with the hope that she would finally pull it together. Unfortunately, with every failed ball contact, her confidence chipped away until she had to be replaced by a substitute who was considered a weaker player. Sitting on the sidelines, she burst into tears, in complete disbelief about what had happened.

I decided to intervene, and we struck up a conversation about what was happening. She cried, "Coach, I don't get it. I've tried so hard, but nothing's working. I can't hit the ball. I can't jump as high as usual. I'm just not playing well. I feel like I'm letting my team down." I asked her a simple question: "What time did you have lunch?" She replied, "I didn't have lunch. I was too nervous." "How much water have you had today?" I asked. "Just this one water bottle," was her answer.

Clearly, she was dehydrated and almost certainly suffering from low blood sugar. I gave her an energy drink plus an additional bottle of water and an energy bar to eat. She sat out the rest of the first set, eating and recovering. By the time the second set started, her energy levels had begun to rise as the food and fluids fueled her brain, nervous system and muscles.

Once fully refueled, she bounced back out of her seat and was ready to play again. During the second and third sets, her performance improved markedly – and with her help, the whole team began to work as a finely tuned machine again. This allowed them to finish the game, tournament, and the year with a victory. The team walked off the court that day with a win they deserved, and after the game, we reconvened for a debriefing. We discussed what went well, and what they felt didn't go well.

Some of the girls recognized that when the team had moments of struggle, such as with the player who suffered from dehydration and missed every ball, they allowed self-defeating thoughts to dominate their own mindsets – about the game, themselves, the other team and even the team member who wasn't playing well. This in turn drove team performance down even further, which in turn could have cost them the first set of the game.

The whole team recognized that the physical *and* emotional state of just one team member can greatly influence the emotional state of all others – and that team performance can drop considerably when the remaining team players allow self-defeating thoughts to take over. The lesson for this team that day was that no matter how well you prepare, or how hard you train, if you don't take care of yourself, not only will your individual performance suffer, but so too will the performance of the whole team.

Since that day, each of the girls has been extremely diligent with her nutrition and exercise. My daughter, who wishes to improve her vertical jump and has a dream of playing at elite levels one day, refers to healthy food as "jump food." She has learned from firsthand experience how her performance – and her team's success – is affected by her own food choices.

This is just one example of the many amazing life lessons to be learned through team sports, and after four years of research, I've learned that it's a crucial lesson for corporate team performance as well. A team-sport athlete understands something important that most office workers don't: we're all part of an ecosystem, and our actions (and inactions) affect the whole team. Every team-sport athlete understands that for the ecosystem to maintain a healthy balance, every athlete needs to bring his or her A-game on a consistent basis.

This is so obvious for sports teams because the consequences of poor individual performance are immediately palpable, as in the case of my daughter's volleyball team. If one player is underperforming, the rest of the team will feel it, and they will likely need to pick up the slack to compensate for one player's subpar performance.

Real ecosystems function this way as well. Think about nature and global warming. Consider what happens when we chop down trees in the Amazon forest. Less oxygen from fewer trees causes carbon dioxide (Co2) levels to rise. The Co2 blocks off the ozone layer, which causes temperatures to rise, which then causes icecaps to melt, which causes water levels to rise, which then precipitates hurricanes all over the world. By messing with the trees in the Amazon forest, we can create hurricanes off the coastlines of Japan and the United States – causing billions, even trillions of dollars in damage, not to mention loss of life.

Now, let's apply this analogy to an organization. Imagine a financial department in Paris with one co-worker who doesn't feel like doing her job. This could possibly affect a salesperson in India. Within today's spread-out global organizations, it's easy to become divorced from our impact, unaware that our attitudes and behaviors are affecting others in the organization – possibly on a different continent. And yet, we do have that impact.

The analogy of an ecosystem goes even further to include our internal environments as well. In fact, internally we *are* an ecosystem. We are a collection of trillions of cells that interact with one another and affect each other in much the same ways as the trees in the Amazon forest affect global temperatures.

When I was studying complementary medicine for my undergraduate degree, we learned that the body consists of numerous systems – the cardiovascular system, the pulmonary system, the skeletal system and so on – yet we learned to treat the systems separately. We learned to treat disease within the realm of that specific system *without necessarily looking outside of that system.*

However, as living human beings, we are much more than the sum of our parts. We are a collection of systems working intricately together. What we do with our intestinal systems can affect the arteries in our hearts. Thankfully, today many more medical practitioners are using sophisticated and holistic approaches to healing and health. The reason for this paradigm shift is that doctors, too, are learning that real healing only occurs with a multidisciplinary approach that targets the whole patient – the whole ecosystem – not just one system within the patient.

Organizations today operate based on similar principles. Managers tend to manage individual systems, even though those systems collectively make up an organization. Each of these systems has a direct effect on all the others, as in any ecosystem. In the same way that the body consists of trillions of cells all working together and influencing one another, so do organizations. Organizations do not literally have cells; however, the "cells" are human beings all influencing one another.

Because all individuals are unique with their own brains and their own thoughts, the complexity of creating emotional cohesion increases exponentially with the size of an organization. Of course, that doesn't mean the systems approach doesn't work at all. Organizations have been functioning with this approach for decades, and most organizations can still do a decent enough job that way.

In modern medicine, too, the systems approach certainly isn't without benefit; it has healed many people over the past few hundred years. However, modern advances in medicine are teaching us that the systems approach can only take us so far. If we want to improve the effectiveness of modern medicine beyond its current scope of performance, we need to turn to complementary approaches that help raise the quality and effectiveness of care.

Likewise, if we want to improve the effectiveness of current organizational management approaches so we can continue improving organizational performance, we need to seek out complementary approaches that add value and increase effectiveness. And one of the keys to finding new approaches is in the understanding of ecosystems and interdependence.

Health and Organizational Performance

In 2013, the Aberdeen Group published its human capital management trends report. The report's general message shared that we need to focus on our people, because as organizations invest in systems and more efficient technology, human capital is being reduced.

Moreover, for the first time ever, our talent is expected to execute multiple functions simultaneously in order to keep costs down to a manageable level. In our efforts to keep those costs down and keep profits high, we are creating a different type of executive – one who performs multiple tasks. But how is the typical executive coping with this shift? Multifunctioning is putting enormous strain and extra stress on executives, who are desperately trying to keep up with increasing demands at work while simultaneously trying to hold on to sanity in their private lives as partners, spouses and parents.

Because of this phenomenon, we're seeing an alarming number of executives suffering from burnout and presenteeism. If you're unfamiliar with the term, "presenteeism" refers to people showing up to work exhausted, depressed or ill. They're present, but they lack the capacity to maintain decent quality work output. We're starting to see stress, anxiety and depression manifesting as medical conditions, resulting in personnel dropping out of organizations because they are not capable of keeping up with the mounting pressure.

Whether we like it or not, people can be either a viable source of revenue or they can be an organization's greatest liabilities. The Aberdeen Group report emphasized the dire need to invest in people, so that they can remain a reliable source of productivity and profit. What this research and other reports are telling us is that these three areas – stress, happiness and performance – are intricately linked. And the balance between them affects the whole organization. The higher the levels of stress, the greater the chances that people aren't going to be happy. When people are not happy, they're not going to perform very well.

Not so long ago, the idea of a happy employee was considered a "soft," touchy-feely, not-so-serious concept. It was believed that we don't have to be happy to be productive at work. But we now know that happy employees are way more productive than unhappy employees.

Happiness is actually a viable source of income for a company. If people are happy, they're going to have more positive attitudes toward work, resulting in improved performance.

The close link between health, happiness and stress is illustrated by the health-performance pyramid, which I initially designed while training elite athletes, but have since adopted for executives as well.

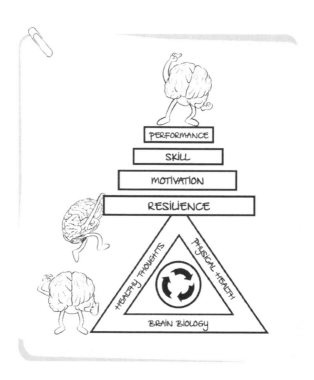

At the bottom of this pyramid is a small triangle that represents our brain biology. Our brain biology is responsible for neurochemicals, the amount of oxygen and hydration in our brains, and many other biological variables. If our brain biology isn't balanced, it significantly affects every aspect of the mind and how it functions: our thoughts, feelings and behavior. That, in turn, is going to affect our health behaviors and the decisions we make about our health. It will impact our diet and exercise choices – which will impact our brain biology, creating a negative feedback loop (also known as a vicious cycle).

Say one night you have a high-fat meal and a lot of alcohol. There's no way your brain is going to have optimal biology the next day. It's going to affect your thought processes, feelings and behavior.

It might influence your thoughts and feelings to the degree that you might *again* choose to have more unhealthy food and alcohol. Which will further degrade your brain biology ... and so on.

On the other hand, if you flip that equation around and really take care of yourself, you will generally have great brain biochemistry, and will function far better. Your thoughts, feelings and behavior are much more likely to be positive. And this, in turn, leads to healthy choices that further support good brain biology – a *positive* feedback loop. And another thing – if you take care of yourself you will have more energy. And energy is critical, because it gives you the brain biology to be resilient.

People who exercise and take care of themselves generally have a lot more energy. They tend to feel that they can cope with whatever is thrown at them. If they get knocked down, they can get straight back up. They have bounce-back ability. That's a large part of the meaning of resilience.

Without energy, we're running on empty. Conversely, if we have a lot of energy because of good health choices, we have reserves. In fact, there's a concept called Cognitive Reserve that suggests we have a limited amount of energy available to us, and it can be either depleted or kept in reserve. Our energy reserves can be used for all sorts of activities, from socializing to sports – that actually recharge our batteries and generate more energy.

Stress, which will be discussed in greater detail in the next chapter, is created when our brain's energy levels deplete. We *feel* unsafe because our brain is running out of gas, and that's considered unsafe by the brain. So the brain goes into survival mode, causing a cascade of effects and outcomes we'll explore.

Energy, cognitive reserves and resilience are important because not only are *you* going to be more proficient and confident – you'll inspire others to higher levels of proficiency and confidence. Your energy "rubs off" on those around you. Additionally, increased proficiency improves performance. These factors are all intricately linked.

I like to call this "the iceberg effect." When we measure performance in executives, we tend to look at the top two layers of performance on the health-performance pyramid. We don't really look at what underlies that behavior – what's underneath the so-called tip of the iceberg – because it isn't easily visible. Because we don't see the brain directly, we don't pay attention to it.

It's important moving forward in different management systems that we consider the deeper neurological levels of functioning and take them into account. If we see a person's performance dropping, it could very well be that the problem is an unbalanced brain. Trying to approach the performance problem at a structural, external or otherwise strictly rational level might not necessarily work. We have to focus on the whole human being.

Health and Employee Performance

Engagement is a popular buzzword these days. According to Scarlett Surveys International, employee engagement is a measure of employees' positive or negative emotional attachments to their jobs, colleagues and organizations. Engagement profoundly influences an employee's willingness to learn and perform at work. So a more engaged employee is more inclined to think on behalf of the organization, team and colleagues.

What about somebody who is disengaged? He'll think only about himself. According to neuroscience, disengagement is actually our default brain state. Thinking selfishly is normal. The brain is designed to be selfish. Selfishness is a survival mechanism that ensures our existence on this planet.

Should we really call a person "disengaged" when he or she is merely doing what biology dictates – to put his or her interests before the organization's interests? What does it accomplish to label as a negative what the brain does merely in its natural attempt to survive? I believe one of the major flaws in leadership is that many of us tend to assume or expect our employees to be engaged *by default*. We shouldn't expect our employees to be *naturally* engaged. We need to take responsibility for their engagement.

If we as leaders are seeking to improve engagement in our employees, it's up to us to ensure that we shape and change brains so they become engaged. We need to apply innovative leadership strategies to ensure that an exceptional level of engagement is attained. And if engagement drops, it's our responsibility to make sure it rises again.

Why is this so important? Research suggests a number of things happen when people are engaged. Concentration levels go up, distraction time goes down, and productivity, creativity and the ability to communicate all increase. Additionally, when people are engaged, their positive personal affect also increases. *Personal affect* is the impact we have on others. When a person walks into a room, one of two things can happen. He or she can suck all the energy out of the entire room. That's what I like to refer to as an "energy vampire." Alternatively, when a person walks into a room, energy levels can soar, seemingly for no reason at all.

His or her presence makes everyone feel amazing and energized. That's positive personal affect.

I'm sure we've all witnessed engaged employees. They're super-excited about what they do, and have more of a positive effect on those around them than people who are disengaged. They're also more emotionally and psychologically resilient, and they improve organizational vitality and adaptation. Employee engagement impacts a marketplace in which billions of dollars are transacted each year. The fact is, a great deal of money can be made or lost based on employee engagement levels.

Earlier, I mentioned the term "presenteeism," referring to the phenomenon of someone who might be physically but not mentally present at work. We now know that presenteeism costs organizations *six* times more than absenteeism. So the people who take extra sick days aren't the only ones organizations should be concerned about. We do need to be concerned about absentees, but presentees are costing organizations much more, not only because of their own lack of productivity, but because they affect the team. Their disengagement cascades down through the entire organization.

So: disengagement – the default state of the brain – has a negative effect on organizational performance and the bottom line. If we as leaders don't introduce initiatives to improve engagement, we can safely assume that employee engagement – and with it organizational performance – will remain far from optimal.

If you're a manager or business owner, chances are good that you're already aware of this issue and are implementing all sorts of employee engagement initiatives to counter it. But there might be a key you're missing in your efforts. Our research, as well as research by other reputable organizations, has shown a clear link between *physical health* and employee engagement. That's right – a *healthy* employee is, in fact, a much more engaged employee.

In 2010, leading global professional services company Towers Watson discovered that people who are engaged also naturally tend to make better health choices. They are more inclined to say, "Hey, I'm really engaged in what I'm doing, I really want to be here and I find this really important. Therefore, I will take care of myself so I can keep engaging." People who are healthier also tend to have a lot more energy, feel happier, expend less energy completing tasks, have lower levels of stress and handle challenges better.

Health as a Viable Business Strategy

Since health is proving to play a vital role in employee engagement, it should not be ignored as a valuable tool in any employee engagement strategy. Two years ago, Gallup surveyed more than a million employees. They discovered that organizations with higher employee engagement actually generate 47 percent more revenue than companies with average or disengaged employees.

47 percent more revenue!

If I could prove to companies that I have a software program to help them earn 47 percent more revenue, every one of them would be interested. Yet in many organizations, employee health is still not considered a high priority or a viable strategy to raise the bottom line. However, data shows a close link between employee health and the actual amount of money organizations make. Health, therefore, represents a viable business strategy, not just something that's nice because it's good for people.

51

Good health practices can actually improve employee engagement and help raise the organization's bottom line.

While I was conducting research in 2010, I had a meeting with the HR Director of American Express. Just like so many large financial organizations, they too suffered greatly after the 2008 financial crash. Interestingly, however, American Express experienced a very low employee turnover, compared to many other organizations.

During our meeting, the HR Director told me that American Express had initiated a very comprehensive employee wellness program prior to the 2008 crash. As a response to the crash, American Express was forced, in many cases, to lower salaries and cut the benefits of many executives. As the American Express leadership team braced themselves for a large exodus of their key executives, to their surprise, many of the employees chose to stay on and worked through the crisis instead.

Amazed by this, the company wanted to know why, despite these serious cutbacks, their employees stayed on. So they conducted a survey in 2010. Astonishingly, the number one reason employees gave for staying and working through the 2008 crash with lower salaries and benefits was that American Express did not cut back on their wellness program during those challenging times. Specifically, the employees said the wellness program made them feel that the company cared about them.

As employees, customers or executives, if we feel that the organization "has our back," we're going to stick with it. If we show our employees that we really care, employee turnover drops.

How much money did this company save as a result of the employee loyalty driven by their solid wellness program? Let's put it into perspective. I'll use McDonald's as an example. An employee at McDonald's in the United States makes about $9 an hour, which comes to around $1,500 dollars per month. How much would it cost McDonald's to actually lose a $9 per hour employee, then rehire and train a replacement?

Based on research conducted by Center for American Progress (CAP) in 2012, to replace a minimum-wage employee costs approximately 20 percent of that employee's annual salary, or about $3,000, if we factor in hidden costs such as productivity loss, recruitment, training, onboarding and so on.

If the cost of employee turnover is 20 percent of an employee's annual salary, what would it cost to replace a $250,000-a-year executive? Well, CAP researched this as well, and they discovered that replacing an executive is a much more costly affair. Through their research, they calculated that it would cost a staggering 216 percent of an executive's annual salary. Imagine how financially draining that is for an organization with a moderate- to high-turnover rate. And imagine the impact on the company's bottom line if we could bring that replacement cost down, even by just 10 percent.

Health and Maslow's Hierarchy

With costs like these at stake, being concerned about employee health and fitness isn't just about compassion or compliance. It's actually an organizational strategy to drive down costs and increase profits, while simultaneously offering an invaluable service that gives employees a feeling of safety. And it turns out that making employees *feel* safe and cared for improves performance – and thus the bottom line – in more ways than one.

A wellness program doesn't just improve employee health directly. The feeling of safety is *itself* also essential to organizational performance – a fact that is best illustrated by a famous psychological model called Maslow's Hierarchy of Needs.

Decades ago, Abraham Maslow designed a simple model in the form of a layered pyramid that he called the Hierarchy of Needs. The pyramid depicts a hierarchy of the various layers of human needs, which we can climb as the needs below are satisfied. Right at the bottom of the pyramid are physiological needs. For example, if you were to start to suffocate for whatever reason, you wouldn't be worrying about what's for lunch. You wouldn't be worrying about anything except trying to breathe.

The moment we perceive that somebody or something is threatening what we need, it creates stress. So if we perceive that breathing, food, water, sex, sleep or any physiological fundamentals are being threatened, it creates stress. The same applies to our sense of safety, social esteem and self-esteem.

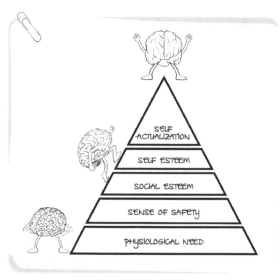

If all layers below are satisfied, and our perceived needs are met, only then are we able to meet a level of self-actualization. Self-actualization is the level at which we need to reside to be creative, to innovate and to relate with others' perspectives. In other words, achieving a level of self-actualization is necessary to be a top performer at home, at work and in life.

The role of health actually presents an interesting conundrum. As Maslow's hierarchy suggests, only employees at the top of the pyramid will have the motivation to exercise regularly and make healthy choices. Yet there's a "which came first, the chicken or the egg" situation (or vicious cycle) here. Unhealthy choices have a direct negative effect on our health. And when health levels decline, it affects our physiological functioning – which is at the bottom of Maslow's Hierarchy.

Ironically, not meeting our physiological needs makes it more challenging to emerge at the top of the pyramid. And good health choices seem to require, for the most part, being at the top level of self-actualization. Practically speaking, our poor health choices one day can put us in more of a "survival mode" situation the next day.

For example, if you end a day on a high note and decide to celebrate with a high-fat meal and more alcohol than the body can metabolize, the next morning will be substantially more challenging for your brain as it will lack essential nutrients to perform at its best. The lack of essential nutrients will make it more challenging for your brain to perceive the world with the same positive perspective as the day before, making you less resilient and more susceptible to stressors that would otherwise bounce off you.

Due to your health choices, you're now responding from a less actualized perspective. In other words, your health choices can actually affect where you reside on Maslow's Hierarchy of Needs.

Health and Leadership

Let's look at this from a leadership perspective. When I ask participants in my workshops about what they consider to be the qualities of a great leader, people typically name the following attributes:

A great leader is someone with vision.

A great leader is an excellent communicator.

A great leader leads from the front.

A great leader is a team player.

A great leader is fair, creative, has great energy, is disciplined and so on.

Of course, these are all great qualities. But more important than merely *possessing* these qualities, is that the people around us *see* those qualities in action. Obviously, as leaders, we need to *have* those qualities for them to be seen. But we tend to underestimate the fact that it's actually how the world *sees* us that's ultimately going to determine how effective we are. It's therefore not just about our qualities but how we demonstrate them that's most important. Our teams should be inspired by our *example*, by *experiencing* our best qualities rather than simply having an idea that we possess those qualities.

Organizations are, thankfully, filled with people who demonstrate inspiring behavior. Leadership isn't restricted to "designated" or "official" leaders. Leadership involves everyone in the organization. In a very real sense, we all have leadership potential and responsibility. Unfortunately, leading by doing can go both ways. Through our actions and attitudes we can inspire positive thoughts and actions, but we can also trigger negative ones, depending on the message our behavior sends.

Let's put this "leading by doing" concept in a neuroscience context.

In the 1980s and 1990s, Italian researchers were doing studies on macaque monkeys in which they were trying to teach the animals to perform certain arm movements. They were measuring brain activity in the prefrontal cortex, the area associated with voluntary motor action. One day, a researcher walked in with an ice cream cone and lifted his arm up to lick the ice cream. As he did so, the same neurons were activated in the monkey's brain and they lit up as if the monkey himself was doing the movement.

What that means is that when I raise my arm, neurons in my brain light up and trigger my muscles – *and if you see me raise my arm, those exact same neurons light up in your brain as well.* The neurons that connect to your parietal cortex are also connected to your visual cortex, thus allowing you to both feel and imagine. So when I raise my arm, in a sense you're raising your arm as well, because – strange as this may seem – the brain does not know the difference between thinking about an action and actually doing it.

In other words, if you see me raise my arm often enough, the part of your motor cortex that's responsible for raising your arm *will actually grow.* My actions have a direct effect on your brain. *I can actually shape your brain this way.*

So as leaders, our actions change the brains of the people around us. We actually change neurons – a process called neuroplasticity.

The implications of this discovery are staggering. If our actions alter another person's brain, for better or for worse, that gives each of us enormous responsibility. This proves that it's what people see us *do*, not what we say, that matters.

In a recent research project, I had the privilege of conducting research on 108 executives in Singapore. In this research, I intended to examine the brain's response to exercise. All participants were first subjected to a series of brain performance tests, after which one-half of the participants were asked to participate in a simple exercise video, and the other half were asked to observe the exercise group working out.

During the exercise segment, I recorded the heart rates of all participants and observers. After the exercise segment, I conducted another battery of brain-performance tests. Participants believed that I was exploring whether or not exercise improves brain function – something that has repeatedly been demonstrated. Participants in the observation group believed that I was only testing the exercisers. However, my actual interest was to see if the *observation* of exercise elicits similar physiological effects as *participation* in exercise.

The exercise group predictably showed that just 12 minutes of mild exercise greatly improves cognitive capacity. However, much more surprising was that 30 percent of the observation group – *the group of people sitting in chairs and watching the exercise group – actually experienced an increase in heart rate.* Here's what else was mind-blowing: those observers who experienced an increase in heart rate *also experienced an increase in brain performance capacity similar to that of the exercising group.*

My conclusion is that the mirror neuron network enabled the observers to "imagine" themselves actually exercising, and it was the imagination of exercise that drove the heart rate to increase. This in turn resulted in the exercise benefits that improve brain function.

These preliminary findings may show for the first time, that when an employee observes his or her leaders exhibiting behaviors such as healthy food choices and regular exercise, it may not only be *inspiring* to them, but *their bodies and brains may actually be experiencing similar health benefits.*

Again, the implications of these findings are far-reaching and enormous. I'm sure it won't take much imagination to assess how having a greater understanding of the mirror neuron network, and how our behaviors affect the health and well-being of our employees, could change the way we approach leadership in other aspects of organizational performance.

Chapter Three

Stress and Performance

"We need to distinguish between stress and stimulation. Having deadlines, setting goals and pushing yourself to perform at capacity are stimulating. Stress is when you're anxious, upset or frustrated, which dramatically reduce your ability to perform."

Andrew Bernstein

A report by the American Psychological Association in 2013 showed that one in five Americans suffers from severe stress. One in five – that's 20 percent of the entire U.S. population, or about 60 million people suffering from stress at any one time.

About 40 percent of Americans reported higher stress today than in previous years – even higher than in 2008 when the economy crashed. Young adults 18 to 33 years old – people many of us imagine are living carefree – now have higher stress ratings than older adults. Almost 20 percent of young adults also suffer from depression. Furthermore, the report showed a strong association between chronic stress, chronic illness and obesity. On top of that, 42 percent of Americans also have stress-related insomnia.

This is a large population of people who are truly suffering. From this data, it's not unreasonable to assume that at least 20 percent of our employees are probably suffering from these sorts of worries and symptoms at any one time, and as a result, are not performing at their full potential.

Symptoms of Stress

Surveys by the American Psychological Association show that Americans attribute their stress to variables such as money, work, the economy, family, relationships, health concerns, housing costs and job stability. Needless to say, stress is taking its toll on our work talent's performance, and that toll may have a much greater cost when we begin to factor in the many psychological and physical symptoms our employees experience due to stress.

In the same report by the American Psychological Association, some of the potentially disabling symptoms of stress listed below are so common, that many workers consider these symptoms to be "the norm" rather than the exception. These symptoms include:

- Fatigue
- Insomnia
- Anxiety
- Inability to concentrate
- Headaches
- Increase in body fat
- Irritability and anger
- Muscle tension
- Lowered immune system function
- Increased disease risk

This shows us that many executives today find themselves trying to perform at their best, but their performance is inhibited by their stress. With such a large percentage of executives suffering from stress and thus performing below their potential, consider the impact this could have on the ecosystem that is the organization.

In my seminars, I often ask my audience how they feel stress affects their personal, but also their organization's performance. These are the answers I typically hear:

Stress causes ineffective decision-making:

It's not that stressed-out people don't make decisions, although procrastination is common. It's more that they don't make the most effective ones.

Stress causes an increase in Negative Personal Affect:

Personal affect is a term to describe how we rub off on each other. Stress reduces energy and tends to put us on the defensive, which can negatively affect the emotions of those around us.

Stress lowers morale:

When we're struggling with our stress and others see us struggling, it can be deeply demoralizing for those around us, in turn lowering their morale.

Stress decreases creativity:

Generally, stress puts us in a completely wrong frame of mind to be able to come up with innovations and solutions to problems.

Stress increases fatigue:

Fatigue and stress-related sleep deprivation have a huge impact on the brain's capacity to perform.

The general consensus of my audience is that they seem to recognize the catastrophic effects stress has on our own performance, but many still don't recognize how the symptoms of stress also increase employee turnover and decrease organizational performance. If a large percentage of the workforce is suffering from stress, it will surely have a negative impact on the organization's bottom line. Unfortunately, the ill effects of stress are not only limited to the workforce. After work, employees go back to their homes, often carrying their stress with them like an infectious virus that affects everyone they come in touch with.

Decades of research by Stanford University's Robert Sapolsky has shown that in baboon families, if the alpha male is having a bad day, he beats his mate. The mate beats her sister, the sister beats her kids, the kids beat their little siblings ... it goes all the way down the chain. And this chain reaction occurs within a very short timespan. The baboon family releases stress by taking it out on other family members.

Interestingly, baboon brains are very similar to ours, so we can generalize these research findings to humans. And indeed, as most of us know all too well, humans do tend to behave in much the same way. Even though many of us won't resort to physical violence when releasing our stress, we may unintentionally act out our stress in an emotional way. When this happens and we act out our stress, we are often unaware we're doing it. And though our behavior might be subtler than that of a baboon, it can still be quite painful for our loved ones. Our words, our tone, our facial expressions, our moods and our demeanor, as well as our actions, can communicate tension and negative emotion, and impact those around us in an insidious manner.

Remember the mirror neuron network in the brain? Our personal behaviors have a profound effect, both physiologically and psychologically, on the people in our direct environments. The mirror neuron network can cause us to actually experience what another is doing – or feeling – by witnessing their actions. This is not limited to our employees and colleagues, but also applies to our families, and indeed everyone with whom we come in contact.

Stress, therefore, is not a private matter. It's an infectious virus that affects everyone in our vicinity. And because it can affect us subconsciously, we are often unaware of the negative impact we're having on those around us.

Stress and Performance

Given all of the above, it's tempting to conclude that all stress is bad. When we hear or read about stress, it usually gets a bad rap. And from everything I've just described, that could make sense. Yet there's more to the story. The fact is, not all stress is bad for us. In many cases, it's actually good for us and we need some stress in order to thrive. To a degree, our ability to manage our stress lies at the foundation of resilience, which in turn lays the foundation for performance.

The concept of a General Adaptation Syndrome (GAS) was coined by famed endocrinologist Dr. Hans Selye back in the 1930s. Through his research, Dr. Selye discovered that there are three phases to adaptation.

The first phase, known as the *alarm* phase, is the physiological response that occurs in response to a perceived stressor. As the brain perceives a stressful situation, it stimulates a cascade of hormonal and neurological responses. These responses increase heart rate and blood pressure (to pump blood and glucose into our muscles), and release stress hormones such as adrenalin and cortisol (that increase our ability to process information at lightning-quick speeds and give us extra strength).

Simultaneously, these physiological changes initiate an anti-inflammatory response just in case we are injured during our escape from the stressor or while we are putting up a valiant fight. This process has also been coined the fight-or-flight response and has been a crucial component in our survival as a species.

The second phase, the *resistance phase*, is the body's adaptive response to a repeated stressor. Dr. Selye discovered that when mice were repeatedly subjected to a stressor, they began to develop a tolerance to the stressor by becoming stronger and more resistant to that stressor. This permitted the mice to recover fully from the effects of that stressor. This has become the foundation of our understanding of adaptation in human performance, both in sports and in executive performance.

Unfortunately, Dr. Selye also discovered that if a stressor is repeated *too* often, without adequate opportunity for recovery, the mice entered a third phase – a stage of *exhaustion*. This phase resulted in maladaptation, and eventually, death.

When we think about stress from an evolutionary perspective, we can see that stress has played a positive role in our adaptation to become who and what we are as humans. Adaptation is at the core of evolution, and stress drives adaptation. Throughout history, whenever we were subjected repeatedly to a stressor – such as a change in climate or food source – we adapted by becoming stronger, smarter and fitter, assuming we had the means to recover adequately from that stimulus. In other words, our survival and our fitness are a reflection of our ability to adapt to change.

When we are in homeostasis – in balance – nothing needs to change and we don't evolve. But nothing in this universe stays the same, except perhaps gravity. In fact, the world – including the business world – is in a constant state of flux, and so is the environment.

Change happens all around us every single day, and one of the reasons we evolved to be the most dominant species on this planet is the fact that we are extremely *adaptable*, permitting that we are given the opportunity to adapt, which, in today's dynamic business climate, is proving to be quite the challenge.

The Brain and Stress

Stress starts in the brain with the *perception* of a stressor, and continues to unfold as the brain initiates behaviors in response to the stressor – along with a cascade of physiological processes in both the brain and body, as described by Dr. Selye. To understand the processes our body undergoes during stress, and their implications, it's helpful to know a bit about brain structure and function.

For simplicity's sake, let's divide the human brain into two brains that are intricately linked. The *limbic brain,* or limbic system, sits deep in the cranium. Think of it as the primal brain. This brain is the size of your fist, and it's responsible for all of our primal behaviors: procreation, eating and fighting for survival.

Wrapped over the limbic system is the *cerebral cortex*, the most recently-developed part of the brain. A critical part of it, located behind the forehead, is called the *frontal cortex,* which contains the *prefrontal cortex*. The prefrontal cortex is your rational, thinking, decision-making brain. It's this critical part of your brain that's able to communicate with other people, to feel empathy for others, to solve problems and to be creative. In short, the prefrontal cortex gives us consciousness and personality.

Without the cerebral cortex, we would function primarily with the limbic brain, and our behavior might be very similar to that of a dog or cat. Compared to the brains of all other animals on this planet, human brains have the largest cerebral cortex relative to our body size, and the greatest percentage of brain (70 percent) dedicated to our prefrontal functions than any other animal, including whales and elephants.

It's this larger cerebral cortex that gives us our evolutionary capacity for adaptation. In addition, this larger cerebral cortex enables us to override many primal behaviors that could be deemed socially unacceptable in today's society and detrimental to performance success. Even though we still feel these primal desires, much of the time most of us can override the desire to act on them because we have functioning frontal lobes that tell us the behavior would be inappropriate.

For example, if our boss criticizes us harshly or someone gives us negative feedback, our primal fight-or-flight response might be to strike back, become defensive or run away. Those would obviously be inappropriate behaviors for a top performer. Fortunately for us, we have that mechanism in the prefrontal cortex that has the capacity to temper those primal reactions. As we will explore later on, that self-control mechanism is at the mercy of our physiology, making it a fickle beast that may work perfectly at times, but other times, may leave us at the total mercy of our limbic "caveman brains," resulting in behaviors that we later end up regretting, and often interfering with a desirable performance outcome.

What we can learn from Hans Selye is that stress works like a double-edge sword. The brain has this amazing capacity to thrive in the presence of some stressors, and actually become more resilient, leading to improved performance. But simultaneously, the brain may completely implode in the presence of other stressors. Much of this has to do with a brain's ability to recover from a stressor, but also with the brain's perspective as to how it views that stressor.

Shifting perspective in the face of adversity may be extremely challenging for the brain, as it requires a great deal of self-regulation. Self-regulation begins with self-awareness, and self-awareness is fueled by knowledge. Let's take a closer look at stress, how we respond to stress, and ultimately, how we can manage our perceptions of stressors.

What Doesn't Kill Us, Primes Us for Performance

Deep inside the limbic brain resides a neuronal structure called the hypothalamus, which is responsible for monitoring and maintaining homeostasis – or physiological balance – within the body. When we perceive a stressful situation, during the *alarm* phase (fight or flight), the hypothalamus initiates a number of hormonal changes that stimulate the adrenal glands to produce cortisol and adrenaline. This is known as the Hypothalamic-Pituitary-Adrenal axis, or HPA axis for short.

Adrenaline activates our muscles, makes our hearts pump faster and gets more oxygen into our tissue cells. At the same time, our pupils dilate so that information from the environment can be scanned and processed more efficiently. The release of adrenaline gives us extra strength and power to deal with the stressor.

Cortisol is released for a few reasons. First, it ensures the rapid release of glucose from the liver, to be used as immediate energy for the muscles and brain. Second, it narrows the arteries to enable blood to squeeze through the arteries at a higher speed (while adrenaline makes the heart pump faster).

Third, cortisol suppresses immune function in an attempt to delay acute inflammation if injury were to occur while fleeing from a threat. Acute inflammation following injury could severely decrease running speed and fighting strength, so it made evolutionary sense to delay healing for a few minutes while we might be fleeing from a predator. Finally, small amounts of cortisol combined with adrenaline also speed up memory processing during a stressful event. This is believed to enable us to learn from the dangerous experience so we can prevent it from happening again in the future.

This cascade of events happens in about 200 milliseconds. So in two-tenths of a second, our bodies and brains are primed to either run or fight. It then takes us a second or two to become consciously aware that we're primed for a fight-or-flight response. In other words, conscious awareness of what's happening in a stressful situation actually comes *after* the brain has responded. That's why so many people impulsively say and do things they quickly regret. Often in a triggered, heated or threatening situation, the brain only becomes consciously aware *after* the action has been taken.

That's how the brain is designed to function. We are *designed* to react before we think – because while our predecessors were being chased by lions, it didn't serve their survival to be thinking about what they were going to cook for dinner.

Unfortunately, of course, that design doesn't always serve us when we're dealing with other humans. Even though this behavior was (and still can be) beneficial in the wild, it also means that a lot of our behavior is reflexive when it doesn't really need to be. The primal responses don't always work at the appropriate time. Sometimes, it's a false alarm. So these mechanisms that served us so well in our earlier evolution have downsides and limitations in modern life.

To understand even further the distinction between good and bad stress and our relationship to it – our healthy/ constructive responses and those less-appropriate responses – we need to consider that there are two nervous systems in the human body: the **sympathetic nervous system** and the **parasympathetic nervous system**.

Think of the *sympathetic* nervous system as the gas pedal when driving a car. When you press the gas, everything starts working – vroom! – and you're off. In a stressful situation, sympathetic nervous system arousal kicks in, and you're ready to go.

On the other hand, the *parasympathetic* nervous system acts like the brakes. When the parasympathetic nervous system is activated, you're actually resting, relaxing, slowing down. In acute stress, the fight-or-flight response is activated. But when you've run away and escaped from the lion and you're safe, the parasympathetic nervous system kicks in. You recover and the body and brain go back to baseline. Now you're ready for another bout with the lion, if necessary.

An amazing thing about the body is that it learns from this experience and finds ways to improve performance – so the next time the lion wants to have you for lunch, you can run even faster. This phenomenon occurs during Dr. Selye's second phase, the *resistance* phase, where you adapt to the stressor. The experience of outrunning the lion makes the tissues in the brain and body stronger and more resilient.

This phenomenon is called **supercompensation**, so named in 1976 by the Hungarian sports scientist Nikolai Jakowlew. With his discovery of this capacity in the human body, he developed a protocol to maximize and capitalize on it for sports, and his protocol has since been adopted by most athletic development programs on the planet. Jakowlew discovered that supercompensation lasts for a while – about four days – after which it starts decreasing. Performance drops back to baseline after about one week.

So if you get chased by a lion once a month, you'll feel lucky to survive. If you get chased by a lion every three or four days, you'll actually supercompensate – and become increasingly effective at outrunning that lion. This is one reason athletes train multiple times per week, so they can remain in a state of supercompensation and continue to improve performance.

Let's now put this into the context of work life and the unique nature of its common stressors. If we had bouts of stress in the workplace every three days or so, it would actually be a good thing. Just like athletes, we would supercompensate and develop greater levels of resilience, making us perform even better than before. So if stress were well-managed and proportional, we would come out on top, performing like super professionals.

The downside comes when we face bouts of stress more frequently or steadily, before we have fully recovered from the last episode(s). At that point, we risk exhaustion, as described by Dr. Selye, because we just can't recover. This kind of unremitting stress, without sufficient recovery and adaptation periods, is what causes both physical and mental/emotional breakdown in many people, whether we're talking about athletes or professionals.

From all of this context, you can see that in reality, stress in and of itself is actually not the culprit. It serves a purpose, as do some of our responses. Our performance capacity from stress is dependent on how we recover. An optimal recovery empowers us to build our bodies and brains, to eventually become top performers, even in the face of adversity. The problem lies in the reality that we typically are not given enough recovery time between stressors, thus resulting in exhaustion and burnout. This is called *chronic stress*, and chronic stress is slowly killing us.

Too Much Priming Kills Our Performance

With drug addiction, a person becomes accustomed to repeated doses of a drug and develops a tolerance to it, resulting in a decreased drug effect. This phenomenon occurs with stress responses as well. Remember the hypothalamus inside the limbic brain that initiates an acute stress response when the brain perceives a stress stimulus? In the case of acute stress, once the hypothalamus receives cortisol produced by the adrenal glands in the brain, it knows that the rest of the body has enough cortisol to function and begins to switch off the stress response. This is typically a very successful system.

However, during the exhaustion phase, when we suffer from chronic stress, the hypothalamus habituates to the amount of cortisol in the body. It begins to develop a tolerance for the cortisol, and decreases its sensitivity to it. When the hypothalamus is desensitized to cortisol, it's less responsive to the hormone, so the adrenal glands continue to produce cortisol even when a stressor is not present.

An unfortunate consequence of too much cortisol in the brain is that cortisol changes us and it changes our brain function – just as estrogen fluctuations can affect a female's sensitivity to the environment, or excessive amounts of testosterone can cause males to be more aggressive. Cortisol is also a steroid, and too much of it affects the way our brains and endocrine systems function.

Cortisol affects the way we think about certain situations. We become more hypersensitive to our environments. We respond more intensely to a perceived threat, and we see threats as larger than they really are. Our blood pressure rises, making us susceptible to heart disease. Our immune function becomes chronically depressed, making us susceptible to infections and disease.

And there's another ironic consequence: although cortisol suppresses inflammation during acute stress, recent studies have shown that chronic stress actually alters the genes of immune cells in such a way that they become *pro*-inflammatory, rather than anti-inflammatory. And inflammation represents a huge and growing health issue. Low-grade chronic inflammation has been associated with every single chronic disease, from heart disease to diabetes to arthritis to many cancers. Of particular concern is the damage these pro-inflammatory cells do to the brain.

Alzheimer's disease, for example, is a disease that gradually kills memory. Previously believed to be a disease limited to the aging population, it's now occurring at much younger ages and is considered one of the fastest-growing chronic diseases.

Chronic stress has been linked with cell death within the hippocampus in healthy individuals. The hippocampus is most known for its memory-processing role and is crucial for optimal functioning, particularly in a leadership context.

Finally, excess cortisol makes it difficult for our bodies to break down body fat, so we gain weight. Simply put, stress physiologically makes us fatter – regardless of the way stress may trigger us to eat. In short, chronic stress, combined with poor recovery, ultimately leads to hyperreactive leaders and/ or employees who are exhausted, have high blood pressure, are gaining weight and risk decreased memory function.

As the name implies, chronic stress is insidious. Because adaptation is in our DNA, the gradual development of chronic stress enables us to shoulder it and yet remain relatively productive in society. Many of us don't notice or see the need to address ill effects of chronic stress – allowing the condition to keep wreaking havoc until at some point we hit a threshold from which we cannot recover.

Our employees who suffer from chronic stress are usually unaware of the cellular damage occurring inside their bodies and brains. Additionally, the large percentage of executives with chronic stress creates a culture where chronic stress is considered the norm rather than the exception. However, as body/brain damage mounts, performance capacity gradually decreases. It takes increased effort to produce the same results as someone who does not suffer from chronic stress.

The gradual decline in performance capacity, combined with increased levels of fatigue, take their toll on any executive despite the best of intentions. Often, the final alternative is either leaving the company, or long-term medical care for a condition called *burnout*. Burnout is generally defined as "a state of mental and/or physical exhaustion caused by excessive and prolonged stress." In 1996, researchers Girdin, Everly and Dusek further subdivided Dr. Selye's exhaustion phase into three sub-phases: the *stress arousal phase*, the *energy conservation phase*, and finally, the *exhaustion phase*.

Most of us have spent some time in the stress arousal phase, when we're just a little bit more irritable, feel a little more anxious, experience periods of high blood pressure, have trouble sleeping, become a bit more forgetful and possibly have more frequent headaches. Usually, we're able to recover from this phase with some time off.

Once we get into the energy conservation phase, however, things get a lot more serious. We begin to isolate ourselves from others, we become more irritable, we become cynical at work and we begin to self-medicate with substances such as alcohol or food. The exhaustion phase is when we actually hit clinical anxiety and depression, experience a serious loss of sex drive, suffer from chronic fatigue and possibly even have thoughts of suicide.

Although most people in industrial nations probably experience burnout at some point, there are two populations of people we can examine who tend to suffer from extreme burnout. The first group consists of executives, and the second group consists of athletes. When burnout happens in an athlete, we don't refer to it as burnout, but rather as *overtraining syndrome*. Yet the symptoms and physiology are exactly the same for an athlete as they are for an executive.

Recovery from burnout requires serious medical treatment, and it can take months for an individual to fully recover. From extensive experience training athletes, I can tell you that most athletes actually don't suffer from overtraining, but more from *poor recovery*. If the recovery strategies from their training are not followed with the same dedication as their training, overtraining syndrome often ensues.

What we can learn from all this is that chronic stress and burnout, with all their disastrous effects, are preventable and reversible – providing that a solid recovery strategy is in place each time we encounter a stressful situation.

Of course, in today's business world, we can't expect ourselves to take a vacation every time we have to deal with a stressful situation – and as we've now seen, effective recovery doesn't require downtime after every little stressor. As we've learned, we can adapt to and even improve from periodic stress punctuated by recovery. It's the chronic unremitting stress with no recovery time that costs us the most.

It would make sense to find strategies to beat stress and improve resilience at work – so we can dramatically increase organizational performance, decrease healthcare costs and reduce employee turnover rates.

Chronic Stress, Weight Gain and Performance

As I mentioned earlier in Chapter 2, our employees' and colleagues' health is deteriorating at an alarming rate, with obesity levels soaring. And if we place data from population studies on obesity and stress side by side, we see a strong correlation between the two. Weight gain is one of the disastrous symptoms of stress. Worse, the ill effects of stress-related weight gain span far beyond a larger waistline to decreased performance capacity.

As mentioned earlier, chronic stress results in chronic cortisol production, which during the exhaustion phase has its own detrimental effects. However, cortisol's effects are not only limited to the brain. Cortisol also triggers a metabolic response in the body to provide the body with glucose during times of starvation.

During our early evolution, cortisol no doubt saved many lives during times of hunger, when food sources were scarce. Thanks to this evolutionary gift, cortisol enables us to manufacture glucose from protein, which we can then use to survive for extended periods of time.

Unfortunately, the protein that is used to generate glucose comes from lean muscle, resulting in muscle-wasting and a decrease in lean mass. This in turn results in a decrease in metabolism (since muscle mass is the "engine" of our metabolism), making us actually more prone to gain body fat even when we eat normal amounts of food.

The damage does not stop there. Elevated cortisol also promotes weight gain by indirectly forcing the liver to convert any food consumed into body fat, which is then stored. Generally speaking, people who gain weight from the effects of stress tend to accumulate most of the fat around the waist. It's well documented that excess belly fat is one of the most dangerous markers, correlated to a host of other serious health conditions.

Furthermore, research conducted in 2013 and published in the International Journal of Obesity showed a direct link between cortisol levels and increased appetite after a stress test. What this means is that cortisol not only slows down our metabolisms by decreasing lean muscle mass, it creates a tendency to eat more, which further promotes unhealthy fat gain.

Besides cortisol, another substance worth discussing is Neuropeptide Y, which is produced by the adrenal glands at the end of a stressful experience. After release by the adrenal glands, Neuropeptide Y ends up in the hypothalamus within the brain, and it triggers a craving for high-sugar and high-fat foods. The evolutionary theory behind this is that after outrunning or outfighting a predator, the body and brain are starved for energy, so the brain shifts its focus to replenishing energy stores as soon as possible. Therefore, it craves high-calorie foods that are quickly absorbed into the bloodstream. In addition, in the body's attempt to retain energy stores for a "rainy day," Neuropeptide Y enters into fat cells, making these cells resistant to fat reduction.

In real-life terms, this means that after we have perceived something as stressful, we're going to experience an increased desire for junk food, *and* our fat cells become resistant to weight-loss behaviors such as exercise and healthy eating – again, a devastating combo.

The end result of all this is a strong proclivity toward weight gain, as all of these factors working together will push our bodies toward slowed metabolism and fat conservation even if we otherwise try to eat healthy and exercise regularly.

Over the past decade or so, a great deal of research has been conducted on the relationship between obesity, brain health and brain performance. The results of this research are quite alarming.

One of the largest research projects to date examined MRIs of more than 700 morbidly obese individuals in 2012. What the researchers discovered was a positive correlation between degree of obesity and decreased brain function. In particular, older obese individuals showed a significant decline in brain performance as compared with non-obese individuals. This means while we may not notice a marked decrease in performance while we are young adults, progressive body-fat gain over the years can reduce our cognitive capacity significantly.

This obviously has many negative connotations and potential consequences, but from a business point of view can certainly put us at a performance disadvantage with younger competition in the workplace. If your goal is to outperform people much younger than you, it's almost certainly critical to stay lean.

The good news about all of this is that in spite of the deleterious effects that stress has on body fat and fitness – and in turn, cognitive performance – these effects do seem to be reversible. For example, additional research conducted over the past two years on morbidly obese bariatric patients, who initially showed a marked decrease in brain capacity, demonstrated significant improvements in brain function as they lost weight after surgery.

Excess body fat and obesity may well cause a decrease in brain capacity and performance, but fat loss reinvigorates brain function. Better yet, *staying* fit, lean and healthy in the first place can keep us functioning and performing optimally before decline begins.

It's What We Make of it That Counts

In her groundbreaking 2002 article in the Harvard Business Review called: "How Resilience Works," Diane Coutu wrote that resilience describes our ability to bounce back from adversity. She posited that resilient people tend to exhibit the same three characteristics: "a staunch acceptance of reality; a deep belief, often buttressed by strongly held values, that life is meaningful; and an uncanny ability to improvise."

In that article, Coutu explained that while many give up in the face of adversity, some people have the uncanny ability to rise to the occasion and emerge victorious. These resilient individuals tend to view the world and their adversity differently than many of their peers, which in turn results in great success where others fail.

Ancient Greek philosopher Epictetus once said: "Man is not moved by events, merely his view of them." We already knew 2,000 years ago that many of us confuse perception with reality. Two of us can witness the same event, but we don't necessarily *feel* the same way about what we see. Much of the time, we don't even "see" the same thing as the next person, even as we gaze upon the same actuality. Are we therefore seeing with our eyes, or are we seeing with our brains?

In neuroscience, perception is defined as "the subjective interpretation of sensations by the brain." In other words, what we see is the brain's *interpretation* of what we are looking at. And this interpretation is heavily influenced by our genetics, memories and our imagination, which results in a *perspective* that is often misinterpreted as reality. For some of us, we tend to look at our world, and events in it, from a glass-half-empty perspective, or with a negativity bias, yet others see their world from a glass-half-full perspective, or a positivity bias.

In business and in leadership, having a staunch acceptance of reality can therefore be heavily influenced by how our brains are biased to seeing our world. Unfortunately, many of us have a stronger bias toward seeing the glass half empty than half full. We can blame this on our evolution, as seeing the world from a negative standpoint allowed us to outlive our predators and adversaries.

Imagine living on this planet 100,000 years ago. On your daily stroll with your tribe's people, while foraging for food in the savannah, you hear the bushes rustle. Maybe half of your tribe's people think, "Hey, that must be our friend, Hank." The other half, however, think this noise could be a lion, which stimulates the fight-or-flight response. They utilize their newfound energy and strength to quickly climb the nearest tree – and then watch Hank's friends get eaten by a lion.

The field of evolutionary psychology theorizes that through natural selection, we ended up outsurviving those humans who thought of their friend Hank before thinking of the lion. This resulted in a population of humans who tend to perceive negatives before they perceive positives. The theory – now confirmed thanks to neuroscience research – states that the human brain has evolved a bias toward negative information. We're preprogrammed to see bad things before we're able to see good things. This makes sense because threat-avoidance has immediate survival value, and therefore is more important than happiness to the brain.

In fact, research shows that it takes a great deal of energy for the brain to override the negative emotions that stem from a perceived negative stressor, because overriding a survival instinct such as the fight-or-flight response does not have survival value. As noted earlier, a fight-or-flight response when encountering a lion makes total sense, but unfortunately, that same fight-or-flight response will occur in response to an angry boss, an angry customer or even a seemingly harmless remark made by an unsuspecting colleague.

And now we know that we're not only programmed for that negative-seeing tendency, but we're wired in a way that resists overcoming it. This predisposition to seeing our world from a glass-half-empty perspective, therefore, can greatly influence our ability to have a staunch sense of reality, as Diane Coutu calls it.

Even so, if we want to improve our own performance, and that of our colleagues, we need to find a way to turn that negativity bias around by rewiring our brains. Research shows that even though it's challenging, it just might be worth the effort.

Dr. Evian Gordon conducted groundbreaking research on the negativity bias. He discovered that we respond to a negative remark five times more strongly than a compliment. Thirty-five years of research conducted by Dr. John Gottman also showed a five-to-one ratio of positive to negative remarks (PNR) in successful marriages. Dr. Gottman refers to "the magic ratio" as a minimum of five positive comments to every negative one.

Emily Heaphy and Marcial Losada conducted similar research in a corporate setting, showing that leadership teams with stronger PNRs also performed much better than teams with lower PNRs. Unsurprisingly, from a leadership perspective, this means the human brain tends to perform better in an environment that is dominated by encouragement and positivity, which then offsets the brain's natural negativity bias.

So, despite our evolved negativity bias, those of us who can view adversity from a glass-half-full perspective approach adversity as a positive challenge rather than a negative one, which in turn fuels us to endure and succeed where others don't. Approaching adversity as a positive challenge enables us to view our adversity with that staunch sense of reality, combined with a sense that what we are doing has meaning and allows us to become adaptable enough to improvise. This makes us more resilient, as Coutu showed in her 2002 article.

Research stemming back from the 1990s on rats and monkeys, and later on humans, also confirmed time and time again that a positive challenge orientation doesn't just help us perform better, it actually builds our brains. In one landmark study back in 1997, Dr. Randy Nudo and his colleagues observed one group of monkeys that had easy access to food. Another group had to work really hard, figuring out ways to get food and then using motor skills to secure it. The researchers then looked at the MRIs of these monkeys' brains. The MRIs showed that the brains of the hardworking monkeys had grown extra brain cells in the areas required for learning these new skills. The monkeys with easy access did not experience any brain development. The message of this research is: "Challenge builds brains. Having it easy doesn't."

So here we're presented with an interesting conundrum. We know from the previous sections that acute stress is good for the brain, permitting we have an opportunity to recover fully and approach the stressor as a positive challenge rather than a negative one. On the flip side, we also learned that chronic unremitting stress, without adequate recovery, wreaks havoc in the body and brain. It will actually kill brain cells; make us prone to reactive, destructive behavior; cause us to gain fat; and make us vulnerable to chronic disease.

Yet our genetic predisposition to perceive events negatively makes us five times more likely to be chronically stressed. This means we need to be extremely diligent about maximizing resilience if we wish to improve performance and defy our genetic predisposition toward stress. Fortunately, exercise and nutrition offer accessible and robust means to greatly boost our resilience – for ourselves and in our workforce. In the next chapter, we'll take a closer look at how that works, as well as discuss a few exercise and nutrition strategies that may help you build resilience against stress.

Chapter Four

Strategies to Improve Resilience Against Stress

"I think a certain amount of stress in life is good. The stress of just working, which takes effort - I think it keeps you going."

Anthony Hopkins

Exercise and nutrition are well known for their many physical benefits, but their psychological effects – in particular, the significant role they play in building resilience against stress – tend to receive less attention from mainstream media. Yet these psychological and resilience-building effects are no less important. In fact, because of the benefits to the brain, exercise and nutrition are essential for anyone interested in improving mental performance.

Exercise and Resilience Against Stress

Exercise builds resilience against stress in a number of ways. First, exercise functions as an energy outlet for a stressed brain. During our evolution, we typically had to physically chase after food or run away from predators, so there was always a physical component to the stress response we encountered. The physical exertion required during those stressful situations enabled us to effectively burn up the stress hormones that resulted.

In today's world, we often experience stressful situations that do not warrant a physical response. This results in excessive cortisol and adrenaline flowing around in our bodies and brains, even long after the perceived stressor, with no requisite physical outlet to burn off those hormones. Engaging in physical activity that makes us huff and puff mimics the physical activity that aided our evolutionary forefathers in resolving stress. It enables the body to metabolize those hormones, removing them from the brain and body and minimizing the effects of prolonged stress.

People who suffer from depression, anxiety and/or stress tend to feel immediate benefits from exercise, in part for this reason. Another reason is that, during exercise, the brain produces powerful antidepressant compounds called endocannabinoids. Furthermore, it also produces endorphins, a brain chemical that is well-known as an exercise benefit. Endorphins are a powerful morphine-like painkiller and mood elevator.

The result of this wonderful cocktail of effects is a person who feels calmer, has a more positive outlook, experiences more energy and boasts lower cortisol levels (which help to stop or reverse stress-related weight gain).

The benefits of exercise don't stop here. As mentioned previously, after an acute stress response, adequate recovery creates a state of supercompensation in which tissue regenerates to become stronger than it was prior to the stressful experience. (*Chronic* stress, of course, leads to tissue *breakdown*, including the loss of neurons in the brain.)

Exercise is actually, in a sense, a form of acute stress. So in response to exercise, the body and brain produce a number of proteins called growth factors that stimulate the growth of tissue. When we exercise, and especially when muscles contract, those muscles produce a growth factor called Brain Derived Neurotrophic Factor (BDNF). As BDNF flows through the body from the contracting muscles, it enters the brain and stimulates the growth of new brain cells in the areas of the brain that are involved with learning and memory.

Only recently, another protein was discovered that stimulates brain cell growth from exercise. Its name is *Noggin*. Noggin stimulates neurogenesis by activating neuron stem cells that are otherwise inhibited when we don't exercise. Until recently, it was believed that neurons in the brain and spinal column could not regenerate. Slowly but surely, as we are discovering more and more about the existence of brain cell fertilizers like BDNF and Noggin, that old-fashioned belief is being replaced by a new mindset that our brains are capable of much more than we previously gave them credit for. This revelation sparked innovative research and opened the doors to a whole new world of unlimited possibilities and innovative applications in medicine, education and leadership.

Exercise Strategies to Improve Resilience Against Stress

The kind of physical activity that creates growth factors such as Brain Derived Neurotrophic Factor (BDNF) is the type of exercise that makes us sweat and huff and puff. It requires exertion. Research shows that endurance training two to three times a week has a positive impact on BDNF, but so too does the type of resistance training that requires us to contract our muscles and build strength.

Strength training can also raise our heart rates. Research shows that strength-building exercise has cardiovascular benefits similar to endurance training. Strength training that also increases heart rate is therefore a highly effective method of building a resilient brain.

Interval training – a method of exercising that involves short periods of moderate- to high-intensity exercise followed by short recovery periods, is a great way to achieve those physiological effects that build resilience. We can make ourselves huff and puff for a few minutes and take a short break to recover, followed again by a few minutes of huffing and puffing, and so on. This type of interval training actually mimics the physical activity of our surviving forefathers.

In addition to huffing-and-puffing forms of exercise, strength training can reactivate and rebuild not only muscle, but vital movement patterns that have been lost due to sedentary lifestyles. Modern lifestyles have many of us moving less and less on a day-to-day basis. The vast amount of sitting we do is causing reverse adaptation, where our muscles and neurons become weaker simply because they are no longer required to be strong.

Movement Efficiency Training

A few years ago, I developed a training method called Movement Efficiency Training (METmethod). This is a form of training that improves the body's natural movement patterns, which in turn enables us to move in the same dynamic manner as our ancestors. This training program has grown considerably over the years and is now a globally accredited training method popular with personal trainers, physical education teachers and physical therapists.

In my work with executives, I discovered that performing exercises to encourage and develop these natural movement patterns also helps improve resilience. The power of this training program does not lie in its complexity, but rather its simplicity. At the foundation of MET are six simple body-weight movements which, conducted as a circuit, make for a highly effective and complete exercise routine. The circuit does not require any exercise equipment at all, meaning it can be completed pretty much anywhere – even in a hotel room during a heavy travel itinerary.

Let's take a closer look at these six movements:

1. The Pushup:

Our ability to push is a fundamental movement pattern required for many movements in daily life – from opening or closing a

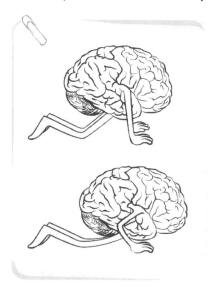

door to catching ourselves in a fall. Much more than a show of strength, the ability to perform a solid pushup throughout our aging process can even add years to our lives. For example, the most disabling injuries in the elderly population are injuries related to falling. In fact, research shows that a broken hip, or even a fractured wrist from a fall, increases the chance of an early death in elderly persons above 65 years of age.

How to perform the pushup:

Begin by lying flat on your stomach. Place your hands on the ground beside your shoulders in a pushup-ready position. Inhale deeply first. At the end of your inhalation, press yourself off the ground into a pushup position while exhaling. At the top of the movement, lower your body slowly to the ground until you are flat on the floor while inhaling.

Regression:

If you do not have the strength to push yourself up fully, focus on what you can do, not on what you can't do. Simply regress the movement – that is, make it a little easier for yourself so that you can perform the movement. One common pushup modification for beginners is to perform the pushup on your knees instead of beginning in a full plank position. Simply bend your legs at the knee so that your heels move toward your back, then push up from your knees only until you've built the strength to do a classic pushup.

Progression:

If a pushup feels too easy, you can challenge yourself by putting more body weight on your right arm during one repetition and then putting more weight on the left arm with the next repetition. This way, you can keep building strength in each arm until one day you might be able to conduct a one-arm pushup.

2. Squats:

Another fundamental movement pattern in daily life is our ability to squat. Day-to-day squatting movements include getting in and out

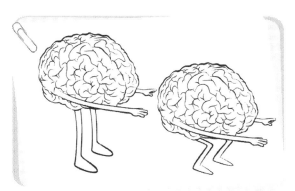

of the office chair, sitting down on the commode, picking up a heavy suitcase and so on. The legs are the pillars of our bodies, and all great structures require a strong foundation.

As I mentioned earlier, chronic stress leads to muscle loss and weakness in the extremities, which includes the legs.

Performing squats as part of an exercise regimen helps minimize muscle-wasting from stress. Also, because the leg muscles are very large in proportion to the body, they require a great deal of oxygen when being exercised, which in turn increases the heart rate. Exercising large muscle groups always offers an excellent cardiovascular benefit. Performing squats as part of any exercise regimen is essential in producing growth factors such as BDNF, and increasing resilience.

How to perform a squat:

Start by standing with your back in front of a chair, bed or bench that is approximately knee-height. Slowly push your hips backward and bend your knees, lowering your body into a sitting position on the chair with your arms stretched out in front of you. While lowering your body to the chair, inhale deeply. Once sitting, lean forward while looking up slightly to ensure your spine is erect. Push your feet into the ground with most of your weight on your heels and stand up forcefully while exhaling. At the top of the movement, connect your brain to your legs by squeezing your leg muscles and buttocks as hard as you can. Once you're comfortable with this movement, remove the chair and perform the exact same movement *imagining* the chair is still present.

Regression:

If you are having difficulty standing up without using your hands, place your hands on your thighs or a sturdy object in front of you, such as a desk. Over time, progressively minimize the support from your hands until you can perform the chair squat without hands.

Progression:

If a chair squat feels too easy, try sitting down and standing up on one leg only while elevating the other foot from the ground. Start with the elevated leg bent, but over time, try to straighten the elevated leg out in front of you. Just as with the chair squat, once you master the movement on one leg, try performing the same movement without a chair.

3. Pulling:

Pulling movements are also essential in day-to-day functioning. Taking a highly enthusiastic dog for a walk or pulling a heavy door open are just two examples of real-life activities in which pulling can be important. Even more important is the activation of the postural muscles in the back of the body. For many executives who spend most of their days in a stooped sitting position, over time the body adapts to this repetitive behavior by rolling the shoulders forward and hunching the back. This hunching weakens the postural muscles in the back and shoulders, increasing the risk of back problems. Having a hunched posture also

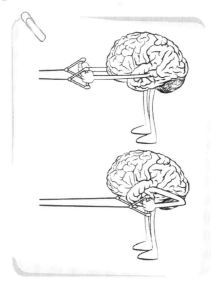

compresses the diaphragm and lungs, thus limiting oxygen intake. This in turn decreases oxygen flow to the brain, thus decreasing performance.

How to pull your postural muscles into shape:

Stand up straight, or sit with an erect spine, with your arms stretched out straight in front of you. While keeping your arms straight, imagine holding onto a rope and pull the rope without bending your elbows, inhaling deeply. The only way you can accomplish this is by squeezing your shoulder blades together.

While you're performing this movement, make sure to keep your shoulders relaxed and pressed down as far as possible from your ears. While squeezing your shoulder blades, connect your brain to your back and squeeze every fiber in your back, from the base of your neck all the way down to your buttocks. If you think you're squeezing as hard as you can, try to increase the squeeze until every neuron and fiber is activated in your back. Once all fibers in the back are activated, bend your elbows and pull your elbows back past your body so that your palms are touching your lowest rib. Inhale even further until your lungs are fully inflated. Once they're fully inflated, return your hands to start position and exhale deeply.

Regression:

If you are having trouble connecting your brain to your back, do not add the arm-bending component. Simply stick with keeping the arms straight and practice squeezing those back muscles. For many executives who have spent many years in a stooped position, these muscles can be severely weakened, and it will take some time before the brain can fully activate those postural muscles.

Progression:

If fully activating the back muscles while pulling the arms back is not a challenge, try performing this movement with resistance bands. While holding one end of the resistance band in each hand, hook the middle of the band around a door handle and step back until you feel a decent amount of tension in the resistance band. Then, perform the same movement, but now with resistance. Stepping away from the anchor point will increase the challenge and stepping toward the anchor point will decrease it. Another alternative is to start with the arms overhead and perform the same exercise as if you are pulling an overhead object down to your shoulders.

4. Lunging:

Another essential movement is lunging, which enables us to walk and climb stairs effortlessly. Adding lunging movements to an exercise regimen will especially help minimize the ill effects of too much sitting. A recent article published in the American Journal of Preventive Medicine showed that sitting more than eight hours per day greatly increases our risk of cardiovascular disease and cancer. If that's not bad enough, anatomy researcher Dr. Robert Schleip of Ulm University in Germany, author of "Fascia The Tensional Network of the Human Body," explains that the connective tissue network called fascia – surrounding our

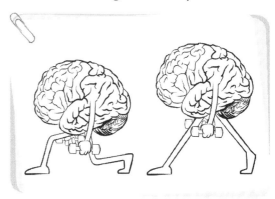

muscles, bones, tendons and ligaments in our legs, buttocks and lower back – is an adaptive tissue that responds proportionately to what we do with our bodies.

When we move regularly, the tissue is thin and pliable, which allows us to move dynamically. However, when we are sedentary, these tissues thicken, and over time, become so thick that they become inflexible, making it more difficult for us to move freely. One can only imagine what the adaptive response would be to sitting for many hours per day. The tissue in our legs, hips and lower back will thicken as an adaptive response, thus increasing risks of chronic lower-back pain and neck pain, which in turn can result in frequent headaches and muscle tension in the shoulders. The good news is that Dr. Schleip's research also showed that when we move, we actually melt the connective tissue back down to its pliable form. Lunges are one exercise that helps to melt down those tissues in the hips, legs and lower back.

How to perform a lunge:

Stand with both feet together in an upright position and your arms out to your sides for balance. Slowly draw your right foot backwards and bring your right knee down to the ground, so that you are in a kneeling position on your right knee and your left leg is bent in front of you. Make sure your upper body is in an upright position with an erect spine, and that your right knee is positioned directly under your hip. Both your right and left knee should be bent at 90 degrees while you are resting on your right knee. If the ground is hard on your knee, place your knee on a pillow, towel or yoga/exercise mat.

While maintaining your balance, exhale deeply, drive your left foot into the ground and put most of your body weight on your left leg. Push yourself up while maintaining an upright posture, without leaning forward, so that your right knee lifts from the ground. Stop when you get as high as possible. Once at the top, squeeze your left leg and left glutes as hard as possible for two seconds to fully connect your brain with your left leg. Once completed, slowly lower the right knee to the ground and repeat the movement.

Regression:

If you are struggling with your balance, utilize a chair or table to improve stability.

Progression:

At the top of the movement, step in with your right foot until your feet are together. If balance is not a challenge for you, instead of bringing your right foot next to the left foot, raise your right knee up in the air in front of you as if you are going to step onto a large step. At the top of the movement, balance for two seconds, then step back with your right foot until your right knee returns to the ground. Think of having to step onto the large step from a kneeling position, driving your left foot into the ground and raising your right leg into the air. Finally, once the movement has been perfected, try adding resistance by holding a weight in each hand.

5. Lifting Overhead:

As with pulling, our ability to lift and raise objects overhead is also inhibited by too much sitting. Adding exercises that enable us to elevate the chest and raise the arms overhead reshapes the upper spine back into its natural position.

How to lift the arms and pull the spine into its natural position:

Start by standing with your back to a wall or door. Raise your elbows to shoulder height with your elbows bent at 90 degrees.

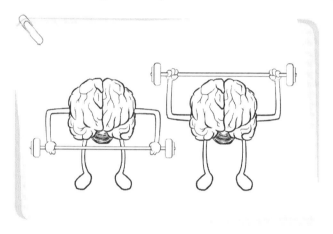

Your hands are open and your palms are facing down while your fingers are pointing into the room. Squeeze your elbows into the wall while your back and legs are not touching the wall. While in this position, keep your elbows to the wall and raise your hands up so the backs of your hands approach the wall. Try to squeeze the backs of your hands into the wall without dropping your elbows below shoulder height. Hold this position for a few seconds and then return back to start position. Make sure to keep the shoulders relaxed rather than elevating the shoulders to the ears while raising the arms.

Regression:

If this movement is extremely challenging, do one arm at a time.

Progression:

Once the hands reach the top position against the wall, slide your arms upward until your arms are completely stretched out overhead. Once you can perform this movement, step away from the wall and try to do this movement holding two dumbbells or a barbell.

6. The Plank:

The final essential movement is actually not a movement, but a stationary position. The plank is widely used in fitness assessments to assess core strength and endurance. Research shows the supreme importance of a strong core musculature. Having core muscles that fire effectively whenever we move is essential to our mobility. Unfortunately, another consequence of too much sitting is that our core musculature is understimulated. As a result, these muscles don't fire effectively when we do move. This in turn can lead to the development of back problems and injuries when we move. Training the core is therefore an essential element in any training program.

Firing up the core:

Even though the plank exercise is often used to practice core endurance, by holding the body in a static plank position for periods of time, we can also use the plank to reignite the core muscles.

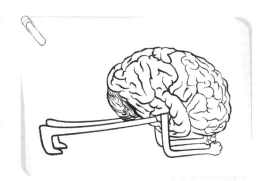

Just as in a regular plank, start by placing your forearms under your shoulders while lying face down on the ground. Raise your upper body and hips off the ground, but leave your knees resting on the ground. Take a deep breath in and raise the knees off the ground. Hold this position for four seconds.

While in this position, connect your brain to your core by squeezing your stomach muscles, side muscles and lower back muscles as hard as possible. Also squeeze the muscles in your legs and buttocks for the full four seconds. To really fire the muscles, try to increase the intensity of the squeeze throughout the four seconds. Then, lower the knees to the ground for about two seconds for a short recovery, then repeat the plank again for another four seconds, followed by two seconds of recovery. With every repetition, ensure you are firing up your core, legs and glutes by squeezing all those muscles as tightly as you can.

Regression:

If raising the knees off the ground is too challenging or causes discomfort, leave the knees on the ground and practice the squeeze exercise.

Progression:

If activating the core is of little or no challenge, try to raise your right arm off the ground, reaching your hand all the way out in front of you, for the four-second squeeze. Do this without rotating the body – keep a level "table" or flat back. On the next repetition, raise the left arm without rotating. The whole time, ensure the squeeze is of equal intensity while you raise one arm off the ground. Once you've mastered this, try raising your right arm and left leg for four seconds, followed by your left arm and right leg, while keeping your trunk in a stationary position and maintaining the intensity of the squeeze.

Repetitions and Rounds

Once you are comfortable with performing each of the above exercises using proper form, you can create a full-body circuit. Simply complete between 12 and 15 repetitions of each exercise, then move on immediately to the next one until you've completed all six exercises in a row. Start with completing just one round of all six exercises, which should take no more than eight to 10 minutes. In time, as resilience improves, increase the number of rounds progressively until you can complete three rounds without rest.

Nutrition and Resilience Against Stress

Probably one of the most underestimated components of resilience is nutrition. Just as an athlete requires a balanced diet with high-quality nutrients to build a strong body, the executive requires the same healthy diet to build a strong and resilient brain. As tissue breaks down from physical exertion during a stress response, it craves the essential nutrients required to regenerate those tissues. Without those essential nutrients, supercompensation after acute stress (such as exercise) is simply not possible.

With chronic stress, excessive cortisol promotes inflammatory proteins that wreak havoc on the body and kill brain cells. A healthy diet minimizes the ill effects of those pro-inflammatory proteins and stimulates the production of growth factors that rebuild tissue.

A balanced diet also provides the brain with the energy and nutrients it needs to function at its best. Just as our muscles require energy to help us exercise, the brain requires a constant supply of energy and nutrients to function accordingly. Without those nutrients, the brain's processing speed decreases and it gradually loses its capacity to perform well. As a result, simple tasks require more effort, leading to greater energy loss, exhaustion and ultimately burnout.

For all these reasons, nutrition is an essential tool for any executive seeking to optimize performance capacity. In the next chapter, we'll look at just how to apply nutrition strategies.

Nutrition Strategies to Improve Resilience

Food is just as important as exercise in creating a fit and resilient brain and body. In addition, being well-fueled by healthy food helps you sustain a healthy exercise routine. After studying human nutrition for years and working with many clients and giving them nutrition advice, I learned one fundamental lesson about nutrition: eating healthy and eating well does not have to be rocket science.

Eating foods that are generally accepted as being healthy, such as **fruits**, **vegetables**, **nuts**, **seeds** and even **lean meats**, will get you a long way. In this section, I will briefly highlight some brain-healthy foods that have been shown to help build resilience in the brain and in the body.

The first foods I would like to highlight are foods like **beans and lentils**, **mussels**, **cottage cheese**, **buffalo meat** (one of my favorites!), **venison** (deer meat), **Greek yogurt**, **eggs**, **tempeh**, **miso** and **raw coconut oil**. These foods are particularly good sources of protein and fat when it comes to brain/body resilience.

Vegetables, too, are a vital part of a resiliency diet because of the vitamins, minerals and healing antioxidants (plant compounds with healthful properties) they provide in addition to fuel. A helpful and simple rule for vegetables is to focus on **dark, leafy greens** – the darker and leafier the better. Dark leafy green vegetables are loaded with nutrients and fiber, and don't add too much to your overall calorie load. Bright orange and red vegetables also offer important vitamins and special phytonutrients.

Third, when choosing a carbohydrate source, such as fruits, vegetables or starches (such as **bread**, **pasta** or **rice**), consider starch choices that are absorbed into the bloodstream at a slower and more constant rate. This is referred to as high-glycemic food, meaning it releases quickly into the bloodstream, or low-glycemic food, which is released at a much slower rate. The slower rate of release will allow glucose to trickle into the body and brain at a steady state, thus maintaining a much healthier blood-sugar balance.

Foods that are high-glycemic, such as candies, cookies, white bread, white potatoes, white pasta and white rice, dump most of their glucose into the bloodstream in one go and then cause our blood-sugar levels to rise rapidly. If the excess blood sugar is not needed by the brain and body, your body will end up storing this excess glucose as body fat. This, in turn, will likely result in weight-gain. An unfortunate consequence of rapidly rising blood-sugar levels is that blood-sugar levels can crash just as quickly, resulting in low blood sugar. Because the brain has limited capacity to store its own glucose, low blood sugar can be interpreted by the brain as starvation, which raises levels of stress in the brain. By balancing our blood-sugar levels by eating low-glycemic foods, we provide the brain with a constant stream of glucose when it requires glucose. This constant stream of glucose will put the brain at ease and help remove levels of stress.

Food quantity is of vital importance to your nutritional picture as well. You need enough food overall, and enough of each type of food – and, conversely, not too much of any of them or too many calories overall. Research shows that when we eat moderate amounts of food and keep our calories in check, we also produce BDNF, the same brain-building protein that we produce when exercising. On the other hand, when we eat too much, or choose processed, unhealthy foods, we produce proteins that cause inflammation in the brain and kill brain cells.

Meals. To start your day, I recommend a great power food, like **oatmeal with raisins and almonds**. Why is oatmeal a power food? Because oatmeal is a low-glycemic source of glucose, that will provide your brain and body with glucose for hours to come. Adding raisins and almonds is not only a great way to add some flavor, but raisins are full of antioxidants that help minimize inflammation in the body, and almonds are full of omega-3 fatty acids that help us build new brain cells.

Why is breakfast important? We have been fasting for six to eight hours or more by the time we wake, and even though we might be in a deep sleep completely unaware of what's happening in our brains, the brain is actually extremely active when we sleep. In fact, research shows that the brain is just as active during sleep as it is when we are awake.

The brain spends those valuable sleep hours reorganizing our thoughts and experiences, and works hard at processing our experiences into valuable memories. Additionally, sleep is the time when the brain stimulates hormone production and begins a crucial rebuilding process after a whole day of continuous fight-or-flight responses. Sleep is essential for our resilience and for building brain capacity, and after a night of sleep, the body and brain are nutrient-deprived and in need of some serious power food to fully replenish.

Skipping breakfast is likely to be detrimental to optimal brain function. Entering into your busy day without quality nutrition may leave the prefrontal cortex starved, limiting its ability to regulate the limbic brain once the first fight-or-flight response comes along. This can explain why you most likely have experienced an inability to concentrate and a tendency to be short-fused when you skip breakfast.

Furthermore, research on the brain's responses after breakfast has shown a significantly greater response to visual stimuli of high-calorie, high-sugar junk food in subjects who skipped breakfast. This makes it even more difficult for you to make healthy choices throughout the rest of your day.

For lunch and dinner, I would recommend meals made up of the nutrient list mentioned earlier.

Water. Water is as powerful and necessary a nutrient for the brain as food. The human body is 60 percent water, and the brain requires a constant flow of water. Major arteries provide the brain with essential nutrients and help flush out impurities. These arteries branch out into tiny capillaries that transport nutrients to the neurons. When hydration is poor, the capillaries close and stop providing the neurons with nutrients and water. Since neurons have limited capacity to store their own nutrients, they soon begin to decrease in function, thus limiting the brain's capacity to perform. During a busy workday, I recommend consuming one glass of water every 30 minutes to keep the brain optimally hydrated and functioning.

In conclusion, building resilience in the brain requires a constant supply of healthy nutrients combined with regular exercise. By following these simple, practical strategies, you will not only build a stronger body, you will especially build a stronger brain that will be more capable of handling the daily grind of life.

Chapter Five

Bob: A Case Study in Stress Management

"Stress is an ignorant state.
It believes everything is an emergency."

Natalie Goldberg

Bob is a senior HR manager at a global company. He is married and has two teenage children, a boy and a girl. He lives in Boston, but spends a lot of time traveling around the U.S. and occasionally to Asia and Europe. His company, which employs 200 people, has several offices in the U.S., two in Europe and two in Asia. The company services the luxury goods sector.

Bob's job is to ensure maximum productivity and engagement from the company's employees who are scattered across the globe. The office cultures vary widely, each reflecting the values of its managers and the country in which it is located. The business has expanded rapidly, and along with the diversity of cultures, this has created a great deal of stress for Bob. He is not only involved in the selection of key employees, but also helped devise and now oversees a new management structure to accommodate the growth of the company. It's a fast-paced job and work environment. To make matters more challenging, the company is a family business, and there are some conflicts between the family members on matters of policy and style.

When Bob first approached me, he explained that he experienced major stress from several sources. At work, his biggest stressor was not so much ensuring that the new management structure was put into place, but rather ensuring that the managers utilized those new systems. This involved a lot of unnecessary dialogue and meetings, which was extremely time-consuming and exhausting. Additionally, not all family members approved of this management structure change, and Bob felt that his efforts were often derailed by family politics within the Board of Directors.

Personal sources of stress included too much travel, fatigue and concerns from Bob's wife that he had no energy left for his family when he was home, which made him feel as if he was failing in both his work and in his private life. This lack of energy, combined with persistent feelings of stress, had recently resulted in weight gain because he just did not have the time or energy to exercise or to be disciplined about his food choices.

Bob and I agreed to start with an initial Headstrong Performance Assessment that would help him determine whether or not his lifestyle was affecting his mental capacity and performance. The Headstrong Performance Assessment combines validated fitness tests, lifestyle satisfaction questionnaires and cognitive function tests. Together, these develop a holistic profile showing the connection between a person's lifestyle choices, health status and cognitive capacity.

The results of his assessment showed that his mental performance, in particular his processing speed and short-term memory, had declined far below the norm compared to his age group. In fact, his brain-processing speed was that of a 70-year-old person, which was a bit of a shock to Bob. Additionally, Bob's stress and anxiety rating was far above normal; he had high blood pressure; he had accumulated a lot of body fat around the trunk; and his cardiovascular fitness was poor.

After seeing the results of his assessment, Bob was keen to make some changes, so we agreed on two strategies. The first strategy was to improve his health and fitness by implementing an exercise and nutrition plan that he could stick to, even if he was traveling. The second strategy was to undergo mental performance coaching to build resilience in the face of his life/work stressors.

Bob's Nutrition Strategy

Bob was under the impression he generally made healthy food choices compared to his colleagues. He always ate a good hearty breakfast, because he understood that breakfast was the most important meal of the day. But like so many of his colleagues, his hectic schedule often interfered with his lunch break, reducing his lunch to a quick sandwich or a pastry and a cup of coffee. More often than not, he didn't even have time for that.

When not traveling, Bob spent afternoons in meetings. By the middle of the afternoon, his energy typically declined to drastically low levels, leaving him feeling exhausted and sluggish. His default remedy to reignite his energy level was to have another cup of coffee or two. Even with the extra coffee, he often felt lethargic and drowsy, which didn't help with his afternoon social interactions and decision-making. That mid-afternoon time was also when he found himself gravitating toward cookies and candy.

By the time he arrived home, Bob was exhausted. He would often have a large meal, justifying this based on the fact that he "hadn't eaten all day." He would then collapse in a chair with a glass of wine to help him wind down. Often, he would fall asleep in front of the TV. He'd wake up after an hour or so and head to bed. When Bob was on the road, his schedule and lifestyle weren't any better. During long flights, he would often consume alcohol to help him sleep. After arrival, he would suffer greatly from jet lag, draining his energy even further.

By not eating for many hours, Bob was depriving his brain of much-needed fuel, rendering it sluggish. As his brain started running on empty, it became less capable of making effective decisions, and processing speeds declined considerably. When

Bob did eat a meal for lunch or dinner, it tended to be high in refined carbohydrates such as white bread, potatoes and white rice. Of course, this did provide his brain with energy in the short term, but did not sustain long-term energy. His erratic eating caused a daily energy roller coaster ride, forcing his brain to suffer greatly during the long periods without nutrients.

Bob didn't consume much water either, and water is essential for brain function. Within the brain is a complex network of arteries and veins that branch out into microscopic capillaries that function as the body's nutrient- and waste- transport system. With dehydration, blood flow becomes more challenging, forcing an increase in blood pressure to ensure that blood can still circulate to all parts of the body.

Unfortunately, as dehydration increases due to a lack of water intake, many of the small capillaries become incapable of supplying essential neurons in the brain with the oxygen and nutrients they need. The capillaries also become incapable of removing metabolic waste from the neuron sites, thus diminishing their capacity to function.

Many executives consider drinking coffee to be a viable pick-me-up. Of course, there's nothing wrong with the occasional cup of coffee, but it's no substitute for good food and adequate water – and when consumed with cream and sugar, it just constitutes empty calories and causes energy levels to drop rapidly. Also, coffee is considered a stimulant that activates the sympathetic nervous system and further increases blood pressure. Bob already suffered from stress, so consuming substances that contributed to the physiological stress response only exacerbated this.

Bob agreed to implement a number of nutritional solutions. First, he would consume meals regularly each day, spaced three to four hours apart, to make sure his brain was receiving energy on a regular basis. Those meals would come primarily from natural, whole foods that are high in fiber, such as fruits and vegetables, to ensure that they would be released into his bloodstream on a more consistent basis. As for protein, he would seek out anti-inflammatory sources such as salmon.

Instead of coffee and alcohol, Bob agreed to drink a lot more water to ensure that nutrients reached the critical parts of his brain. He agreed to drink one 600ml water bottle in the morning right after waking up, one mid-morning, one mid-afternoon and at least one bottle after dinner.

To counter the mid-afternoon snacking, Bob agreed to bring with him to work (and traveling) a piece of fruit and small snack-sized baggies of almonds or walnuts, which he would consume instead of cookies.

Bob's Exercise Strategy

Initially, Bob was a bit intimidated by the idea of doing body weight exercises, since he hadn't exercised in quite some time. We agreed that instead of focusing on what he perceived he could not do, Bob would shift his focus to what he *could* do. This enabled Bob to stop focusing on challenges as being threats, and to start seeing them as brain-building opportunities instead.

He felt that time constraints at work and his low fitness level would not allow him to complete more than one round of the METmethod workout's six fundamental exercises, and he chose the regression versions of each exercise. He completed his six-minute METmethod workout three times per week. On the other days, he would take a relaxing lunchtime walk. He scheduled this walk into his diary so that his secretary wouldn't book meetings during that time unless absolutely necessary.

Over the course of a few weeks, Bob discovered that his stamina was improving. He was able to increase the number of rounds of the METmethod workout circuit progressively until he could complete three rounds. Once he achieved three rounds, Bob discovered that his strength was improving, so he also started to challenge himself by introducing some progressions into the routine.

Bob's Behavioral Strategy

It was important for Bob to recognize that there were inherent challenges in his job, and these probably weren't going to go away. But the job challenges weren't the core problem; the real issue was Bob's ability to *deal with* the stress he felt as a *result* of the challenges. His lifestyle choices only compounded the stress by eroding his brain's ability to deal with it.

Bob needed to learn how to recognize when his brain perceived a stressor as a negative rather than as a positive challenge – and then to shift his mindset to see the stressor as a positive challenge. This required a great deal of self-awareness and practice. Initially, Bob would get so caught up with work that he was often unaware of his stress level until it was too late. By that point, thinking about implementing any self-regulation techniques made Bob even more anxious. We therefore decided to use a different arena in which Bob could practice mental resilience. The arena of choice was exercise.

In much the same way as an airline pilot spends thousands of hours in a flight simulator, learning to master appropriate maneuvers in response to life-threatening situations, so too can an executive use exercise as a simulator to learn appropriate behaviors.

During our first exercise session together, I asked Bob to perform the six METmethod exercises consecutively. The first exercise – pushups – went fine, but as he progressed through the remaining exercises, I noticed that Bob was beginning to fatigue rapidly. He started breathing heavily, his facial expressions displayed exhaustion and in between exercises he would hunch over gasping for air. At the end of the circuit, Bob flopped down on the ground dramatically with arms and legs spread-eagled in a physical display of exhaustion.

When I asked Bob how he felt, his answer was, "Oh my god … that was *horrible!*" Like a pilot, Bob had just experienced his first time in the simulator – and like many first-time pilots, he crashed and burned. My reply to Bob was: "Good. You are now ready for coaching."

We spent the rest of the session analyzing Bob's thoughts and emotions during the six minutes of exercise. Bob disclosed that the more fatigued he became while performing the exercise, the louder his body would scream about its discomfort. He could feel his muscles protesting and burning, his heart racing, and his lungs smarting and stinging. These messages from his body would not only make Bob *feel* uncomfortable, but he would then start *behaving* "uncomfortable" in response to those feelings.

I impressed upon Bob that his body was not "screaming" at him, but merely sending his brain signals. It was his brain that was *interpreting* those signals as screams and discomfort, which in turn made him behave as if he were tired. His brain had turned exercise – something that can be seen as a positive source of growth – into something threatening and horrible. This was a completely separate process from the actual exercises. This was also, in fact, the exact same neural process that Bob endured every day at work. Bob learned that day how his brain gravitates toward perceiving situations as negative rather than positive.

I then took Bob through a process in which he "relived" those signals from the body during each exercise, and I worked with him to identify them as merely signals. This enabled him to separate the *psychological interpretation* from the *physiological signals*. Once separated, the signals no longer had the same impact on his brain.

Bob discovered that he could decrease the intensity of the signals from his body by calming his breathing and making himself relax in acceptance of those signals. As Bob relaxed, breathed and accepted the signals, they decreased in intensity, making it possible for his brain to focus on the exercise rather than on the interpretation of discomfort.

His next step was to learn to see those signals as brain- and body-building signals essential for resilience and growth. We achieved this by having Bob visualize himself doing the exercises while his brain and muscles grew from the signals. The greater the intensity of the signals in his imagination, the greater the growth he would envision for himself.

Seeing those signals as a positive source of growth enabled Bob to go through a second round of exercises. Not surprisingly, this time he steamrolled through them feeling more energized and positive. He continued practicing this skill as he exercised, and over time, he noticed that the signals from his body stopped appearing as uncomfortable. In fact, he reached a point where he actually enjoyed the feeling of those signals. His brain had adapted to seeing the signals as something positive. This was a huge shift for Bob.

The light-bulb moment came when he began to notice how his brain would respond to situations at work in the same way it had done with the signals from the body. He saw that his behavior was often dictated by his negative interpretation of a situation. His brain then made the connection between exercise and work, opening the door to applying the same coping mechanisms at work that he was using in the gym to shift his experience of exercise.

Results

Gradually, Bob's mindset shifted from a focus on threats to seeing opportunities for growth. His physical improvements fueled his confidence to challenge himself more in his exercise, his nutritional choices, and when dealing with challenges at work.

After just a few weeks, Bob's energy level soared. His ability to manage his time and his thoughts improved considerably. With a better-functioning brain, he could actually implement stress management and coping strategies on the spot, which enabled him to feel much calmer and more relaxed during the day.

This had positive side effects. For example, it became much easier for him to understand others' points of view, and he found himself more able to empathize with the pressures *they* were under. This increase in understanding and empathy allowed him to react very differently to others' stress, and left him feeling more in control.

With more energy and less pressure, Bob could relax more. He became much more capable of living in the moment, rather than constantly worrying about all the things he had to do. His wife commented on how much better his interactions with the family were. She and the children no longer felt as if they were walking on eggshells to protect dad. Bob even noticed that he was starting to lose excess fat, which was a very nice bonus.

After just eight weeks, we conducted his second Headstrong Performance Assessment. His score had improved considerably. Not only did he improve on the fitness tests, but his cognitive processing speed improved greatly to a level comparable with others in his age group. Bob himself was amazed that while his workload hadn't changed, his reaction to it had. Not only had his lifestyle changes made him healthier and leaner, but his improved brain capacity enabled him to be a better professional, husband and father.

I am constantly amazed that highly capable executives like Bob allow themselves to get sidetracked into lifestyle behaviors that negatively impact their functioning by reducing their brain's capacity.

The more stressful life gets, the greater the tendency to drop the very practices that are essential for brain health. How many people stop exercising when under stress because they "don't have the time?" And yet exercise is the best stress manager around, and eliminating it at times of stress is the worst thing you can do. It doesn't solve the problem – it compounds it.

Bob's story shows that with a few vital changes in diet and exercise, and key adjustments in the perception of challenge, we can greatly improve the brain's capacity to respond positively to stress – and boost performance in the process.

Chapter Six

Sustained Attention and Performance

*"Concentrate all your thoughts on the work at hand.
The sun's rays do not burn until brought to a focus."*

Alexander Graham Bell

A few years ago, my family and I decided to spend Christmas doing something really adventurous. We traveled to the island of Komodo in Indonesia to see the Komodo dragons.

Komodo dragons are the largest living land dinosaurs. A ferocious ambush predator, the Komodo kills its prey with one venomous bite from its bacteria-infested mouth and then retreats to follow its prey from a safe distance until the prey drops dead from anaphylactic shock.

Unfortunately, the Komodo dragon population has declined steadily over the past decades until it hit critically endangered levels. To protect the critically endangered species, the Indonesian government has gone to great lengths to keep the island as original as possible.

Arriving at Komodo Island, we were met by park rangers who take tourists on guided tours across the island to see these majestic creatures living in their natural habitat. Before we started the tour with our guide, we were informed that Komodo dragons have killed unsuspecting tourists in the past, so we had to stay close behind our guide and travel in single file at all times – all the while keeping an eye out in the bushes around us for any dragons in hiding.

It wasn't long before we saw our first dragon – basking in the sun right on our path. The guide told us that the dragons are cold-blooded, like all reptiles, and that they are generally docile when basking. "It's the dragons we can't see that we need to be cautious of," he said.

We then wandered off along a small bush trail and got to see some other local animals, such as buffalo and goats, which are the staple diet of the Komodo dragon. Walking along a riverbed, the guide mentioned that this was a place many Komodo dragons congregate to hunt and drink water, so we needed to be on the alert.

My wife was walking in front of me. She was looking intently left and right, trying to spot the camouflaged Komodos waiting to jump out at us and eat us for breakfast.

All of a sudden she shrieked so loud it even scared the Komodo dragons. Standing in front of me, I saw my wife standing knee-high in buffalo dung. It was by far the largest mound of dung I have ever seen, and my wife had stepped right into it.

Of course, the rest of us burst out laughing, and my wife eventually joined in. My wife said, "I can't believe I didn't see that. That pile of dung is huge." We then continued on the tour, laughing about the experience all the way back.

What my wife experienced at that moment was a phenomenon coined as *inattentional blindness* by neuropsychologists Arien Mack and Irvin Rock back in the late '90s. This phenomenon has since sparked a great deal of interest from the scientific community.

Inattentional blindness refers to the way in which the brain pays attention only to those things it finds important, and will block out seemingly irrelevant information so we can contribute more brain capacity to what is perceived as important or relevant.

In that instance, my wife's brain prioritized the potential threat of a Komodo dragon attacking her and her family. Therefore, her brain did not register the buffalo dung until she was standing knee deep in it. Fortunately for us, her inattentional blindness at that moment was merely a source of entertainment for us, and did not have any serious negative consequence.

Inattentional blindness can be a highly effective survival tool that allows the brain to expend energy on and apply capacity to what it perceives as appropriate in a given moment, conserving necessary energy. But as effective as this survival tool might be when in the wild watching out for Komodo dragons, or foraging for food as our ancestors did, inattentional blindness can also be destructive.

It can be the executive's greatest downfall when the brain chooses to pay attention to stimuli in its environment other than work. When distractors become the brain's primary object of attention, performance naturally suffers.

This section focuses on the neuroscience behind what the brain pays attention to. Later we will explore how to use nutrition and exercise to train our brains to maintain focus and minimize distractions, which in turn can help us improve our performance.

What is Attention?

The concept of *attention* is familiar to every one of us. We generally know what it means to pay attention to what's at hand in the present. Conversely, I'm sure we've all had the experience of our attention "wandering" to something other than what's in front of us or what we "should" be (or even intend to be) paying attention to.

A classic daydreamer as a child, I have many memories of when I was reminded to *pay attention* in school because my mind was so often clearly on something other than what the teacher was talking about.

We can all think of scenarios in which we experienced a lapse in attention, or found our brains gravitating toward a different task than the one at hand. How many of us have sat in a long meeting and experienced complete lapses of attention, missing major pieces of information, because the brain went for a joyride during someone's presentation?

Perhaps out of nowhere, the brain begins wondering whether or not a specific email arrived, or what you might choose for lunch, or whether you should call your mother tonight, or what to get your friend for her birthday, or so on – any of which the brain finds much more interesting, at that moment, than the presentation.

The brain's ability – or inability – to be fully attentive, has baffled scientists for decades. While we all have our own unique experiences with attention, the concept of attention is proving to be one that encompasses many neurocognitive processes involving many regions of the brain, making it extremely challenging to create a definition for the word.

Addressing the complexity of this term, Harold Pashler wrote in his book, "The Psychology of Attention," that even though everyone *senses* what attention is, no one really knows *exactly* what it is – making it difficult for scientists to develop specific tests that measure it. One consensus shared by virtually all scientists is that attention seems to be a process wherein the brain chooses some information for further processing, while effectively inhibiting other non-relevant information from further processing.

After years of working with brain-injury patients, McKay Moore Sohlberg and Catherine A. Mateer developed an ascending model, or ladder, depicting various types of attention.

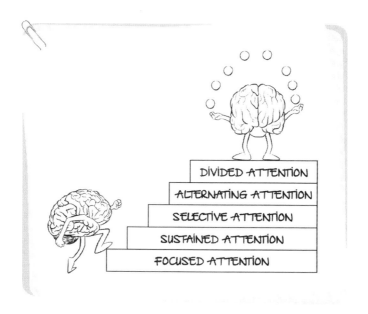

At the base of the ladder is *focused attention*, which is our ability to focus on a stimulus such as a sound or touch. Next up the ladder is *sustained attention*, which is our ability to focus on a task for extended periods of time.

Above that is *selective attention*, meaning our ability to block out unnecessary distractions while on task. Another form of attention is our ability to rapidly switch tasks from one to the other, known as *alternating attention*. Finally, at the top of the ladder is *divided attention*, our ability to complete two tasks at the same time.

Through their research, Sohlberg and Mateer pointed out that as you move up the ladder, each successive layer of the attentional ladder requires a greater amount of cognitive capacity from the brain than the previous one. Our ability to perform well in every one of these attentional layers is essential for optimal performance. In fact, our day-to-day performance often requires us to practice several or even all five forms of attention at any given moment. We always need to be in a state of readiness to pay attention.

Yet the higher we need to climb up the attentional ladder, the more effort is required from our brains to perform at that level. So divided attention (performing two tasks simultaneously) will take a great deal more effort than sustained attention (passively listening to a presentation, for example).

What happens if insufficient energy is available for the brain to exert the regulatory effort required to perform at a particular level of attention? For example, if we skipped breakfast and need to attend a presentation first thing in the morning. Well, if not enough energy is available, performance at that required attentional level will diminish dramatically, making it extremely challenging – if not impossible – to remain appropriately attentive on the task at hand, at that level of attention.

For example, if we need to perform a task requiring divided attention, such as watching a presentation and taking notes at the same time, and the brain's regulatory capacity is diminished because we skipped breakfast, then that level of attention ability will cease and it will become increasingly more difficult to pay attention to what is being said while taking notes.

It may be possible to alternate attention, a lower level of attention, but this would mean that we pay attention to the presentation and then while taking notes, we miss the information that is being presented because the brain has lost the capacity to listen while writing. What this means is that we miss pockets of information from the presentation, as the brain needs to switch attention from one task to the other.

When the brain's attentional capacity drops below the level of selective attention, only focused attention and sustained attention remain. The unfortunate consequence here is that the brain begins to focus on any stimulus that presents itself. These stimuli can be external or internal.

An external stimulus is from outside our bodies, such as the phone ringing, the notification sound that a new email has arrived or a colleague coming over for a quick chat. An internal stimulus is one that originates from inside of us, such as our own thoughts, emotions and physical sensations – such as the need to go to the bathroom, feeling hungry or thirsty, a headache or other source of discomfort.

Attention and Performance at Work

Externally, executives today are bombarded with scores of distracting stimuli. Recently, the "Wall Street Journal" stated that as screens multiply and organizations push frazzled workers to do more with less, the ill effects of distraction create a serious issue that impacts the average organization's bottom line.

Information technology research firm Basex conducted research in 2006 on 1,000 workers, and estimated that distractions consume almost 30 percent of workers' time – costing the U.S. economy a whopping $588 billion dollars per year.

More recently, Gloria Mark, an associate professor at the Donald Bren School of Information and Computer Sciences at the

University of California, observed a sample of workers and recorded their movements for three full days. In her research, she discovered that workers spend on average just 11 minutes on a task before being distracted.

After the distraction, it takes the average worker 23 minutes to finally get back on task again. What this research suggests is that the average worker spends just *22 minutes per hour* working on task! Interestingly, in Marks' study, slightly more than half of the distractions came from external stimuli, while slightly less than half were from internal stimuli.

Compounding the loss of performance from distractions is the amount of valuable energy that's wasted when we shift our attention from one task to another and then back again, which tends to be more the norm than the exception in today's workplace.

Many executives refer to performing multiple tasks simultaneously as being a form of *multitasking*. However, this type of shifting attention between tasks is actually a form of *alternating attention*.

Research now shows that real multitasking is only possible when performing very simple tasks that do not require much attention and capacity from the brain. Tasks such as walking in the park while having a conversation with a friend, or taking notes while listening to a presentation – are forms of divided attention that the brain can handle, permitting the brain has the energy.

But the moment the brain must pay attention to two tasks that require significant cognitive input – such as writing a proposal and reading an email, or driving a car while texting – then the brain is forced to choose which task to dedicate resources to, and ends up switching rapidly from one task to another.

Switching from task to task requires a greater amount of energy for the brain than simply completing one task before the other. The brain must expend energy to disengage from one task, then expend more energy to shift focus, then expend still more energy to engage with the alternating task.

Upon a request from the "New York Times," researchers from Carnegie Mellon University set out to investigate just how much energy is lost during our attempts to alternate attention versus when we single-task. The results of the research were astonishing. The researchers tested 136 participants and discovered that when we alternate our attention, we make 20 percent more mistakes than when we complete one task at a time.

Furthermore, the unnecessary wastage of valuable energy while task-switching is likely taking its toll on our health, as increasing numbers of executives today are suffering from emotional exhaustion and burnout.

A 2012 publication of the International Journal of Stress Management reported the results of research investigating the relationship between employee exhaustion and counterproductive work behaviors. These behaviors ranged from low motivation to complete work tasks, tardiness, gossiping, aggression and sabotage. What they found was a direct correlation between the degree of employee exhaustion and the number of these previously mentioned, counterproductive behaviors – and it affected the entire organization.

Many organizations and executives today still mistakenly value multitasking (which most often ends up actually being alternating attention, or switching) as a benchmark for performance. Yet if we were able to *decrease* the amount of multitasking attempts in the workplace, and replace them with systematic single-tasking approaches, employees would experience greater levels of energy. That increased energy could be expended on other tasks, thus increasing performance substantially.

One of the greatest challenges when deciding to single-task is choosing which task requires our immediate attention. Unfortunately for our brains, what we pay attention to is not always a conscious and calculated decision. Let's take a closer look at how attention works in the brain, for some insights into how we can support the brain's capacity to attend to the task at hand.

Voluntary Attention and Performance

In a recent marketing campaign in Korea, Dunkin' Donuts initiated a highly inventive campaign to capture the attention of bus passengers and get them thinking about buying their morning coffee at Dunkin' Donuts rather than at one of the competitors.

Their strategy was to install machines that would spray the aroma of coffee in the bus at the same time that the Dunkin' Donuts jingle played on the radio. Passengers experiencing this coffee aroma would then associate that aroma with Dunkin' Donuts.

To further solidify the association, large Dunkin' Donuts billboards were placed at the bus stops, pointing disembarking passengers in the direction of the nearest Dunkin' Donuts outlets. As a result of this campaign, Dunkin' Donuts received 16 percent more visitors, resulting in a whopping sales increase of 29 percent.

What these passengers experienced was the result of a new and emerging field in marketing called *neuro-marketing*. Neuro-marketing studies how to capture the brain's attention with marketing stimuli (such as the smell of coffee combined with a jingle) with the hope of evoking an internal stimulus – in this case, a craving for Dunkin' Donuts coffee.

Trying to reach a population of people whose brains are already inundated by external stimuli from a plethora of advertising, companies are always looking for innovative ways to capture our brains' attention. Neuro-marketing may be the next level in the evolution of marketing.

What this example of neuro-marketing shows is that the brain is bombarded daily with all manner of external stimuli through our senses. It must somehow decide and prioritize which stimuli are relevant for processing and which are not, or are less so.

In addition to external stimuli, the brain is also bombarded constantly with information from inside our bodies and brains, such as signals regarding hunger, thirst, physical comfort, emotions and thoughts. These stimuli are all considered internal stimuli.

With all of this information entering the brain, how does the brain maintain sanity and order? It does so by carefully selecting what it deems attention-worthy. This process is a function of consciousness. As you might recall, the subcortical areas deep inside the brain, such as the limbic system, are *subconscious* areas – meaning that we don't consciously perceive what's going on in that part of the brain unless we need to become consciously aware of it.

Consciousness is a process directed by the prefrontal cortex. If the prefrontal cortex is not informed of anything that needs paying attention to, it won't pay attention to it unless it chooses to do so voluntarily. If the prefrontal cortex *chooses* to pay attention to something, it is known as *voluntary attention* or *top-down processing*. On the other hand, if something *captures* the prefrontal cortex's attention, it's known as *automatic attention* or *bottom-up* processing.

According to research conducted over the past 100 years or so, stimuli capable of capturing the attention of the prefrontal cortex tend to represent danger, novelty or the unexpected, or in some other way appear interesting or stand out (saliency).

Imagine being at work and creating an important presentation. As you're staring at your computer screen paying full, voluntary attention to your work, the phone rings beside you. When the phone rings, your brain must disengage its focus on the computer, shift its focus to the phone ringing, and then engage its focus on the phone. The brain's response to the ringing phone could be considered an automatic process.

However, as with all things neuroscience, things are a little more complex than that. Your automatic response to the ringing phone has in fact not always been automatic. Research on babies and toddlers has shown that a ringing phone does not evoke a natural response to pick up the phone. Instead, toddlers continue to play and do not respond to a ringing phone.

Initially, and intrinsically, the ringing of a phone has no meaning for a child. As children age, however, they learn to associate the ringing of a phone with a person on the other line, which piques interest and motivates them to pay attention to and subsequently pick up a ringing phone.

In the same way that Pavlov's dogs learned to salivate in the anticipation of food after hearing a ringing bell, we too can be conditioned to respond to the ringing phone. With repetition after repetition, the brain gradually learns to prioritize the sound of the ringing phone, and develops an automatic response to it, which is a form of conditioning called classic conditioning.

What this means is that our responses to many stimuli in the workplace may be automatic today, but these responses and behaviors were learned through classic conditioning. The good news is that what was learned can also be unlearned through training. Just as we have the capacity to unlearn old, performance-diminishing habits, we also have the capacity to learn new, performance-building habits. Unfortunately, what the brain will pay attention to is also heavily influenced by what state of *arousal* the brain is in, which is heavily influenced by our physiology.

Arousal and Performance

Imagine sitting in a very important meeting with a potential new client. This client will be the largest account the company has ever signed, and you've been chosen to lead the negotiations.

After opening the conversation, it soon becomes a serious game of chess where every bit of your attention needs to be spent listening to and interpreting everything your counterpart does and does not say. Shortly after commencing with the negotiations, you begin to feel a slight signal coming from your bladder notifying you that sometime down the line, a bathroom break may be required. However, the negotiations are so important, there's no way you'll want to excuse yourself from the table.

Forty-five minutes later, the negotiations are still underway, and by now your bladder is screaming out that an immediate bathroom break is warranted. Yet the negotiations are still so intense, there's no way you can leave the table.

You find yourself slowly paying more attention to the need to relieve yourself. You begin to experience moments of inattentional blindness, where your mind begins to wander away from the negotiation and toward the need to go to the bathroom.

This causes you to miss key cues that you could have used to seal the deal. As the need to use the bathroom becomes almost unbearable, it becomes increasingly difficult to even maintain a conversation with your counterpart.

What happened here was that the brain gradually switched from paying *voluntary* attention to the *external* environment to paying *involuntary* attention to the body's *internal* environment.

There are many other internal stimuli, or messages, that can distract the brain from remaining focused on its tasks: hunger, dehydration, fatigue, pain, discomfort, hormonal balance and so on. Any of these internal processes, when poorly managed, can rob the brain of its capacity to focus and pay full voluntary attention to the task at hand.

Remember, the brain is a poor multitasker, so as stimuli become more intense, the brain is forced to pull resources away from the focused task so it can dedicate attention to the stimuli from the body.

Clearly, our physiological state greatly influences the brain's capacity to pay full voluntary attention to our tasks at work. The stronger the physical sensations and impulses become, the less efficient the prefrontal cortex becomes at overriding them.

Extreme effort from the prefrontal cortex to voluntarily stay on task and ignore distractors, either from our internal or external environment, also consumes a tremendous amount of energy, as does any multitasking in the workplace.

An interesting fact about attention is that optimal attention and mental focus reside in what's known as a "Goldilocks zone" (referencing the "just right" ideal in the famed children's story), where the physiology in our brains and bodies needs to be in an ideal state. This Goldilocks zone, or performance zone, is where many influencing factors, such as our hormones, neurotransmitters, nutrients, minerals, oxygen levels and hydration levels, must be perfectly aligned to enable an optimal balance in the prefrontal cortex. This in turn primes the brain to pay voluntary attention to the needed task and override any impulses to pay attention to distractors.

As highlighted earlier, we are biological beings where all of these physiological factors flow through the brain and body, much like the tides in the ocean. These tidal surges push our brains in and out of that performance zone, often leaving us with just a small window of time where we can really enjoy optimal attention in the performance zone. The good news is that our lifestyle choices, such as exercise and nutrition, have a strong influence on our physiology. The better our lifestyle choices, the more we can increase our time in the performance zone, which increases our potential to be fully attentive for a longer period of time.

Outside of these natural factors that influence our time in the performance zone, there are also unnatural influencers that can have a negative effect on our brains' ability to reside in the performance zone. Unnatural influencers can be food additives, chemicals in the environment, cigarettes, alcohol and other drugs that greatly influence arousal levels.

As these factors flow back and forth through the prefrontal cortex, they have an effect on the levels of excitement in the brain, also known as arousal. The drug marijuana, for example, lowers levels of arousal in the brain, making us feel extremely mellow. This could be considered a state of underarousal. Our brains can also be underaroused by a lack of stimulation, which could be referred to as boredom.

On the other hand, a few cups of coffee can push our brains into a state of overexcitement or overarousal, as does the perception of a threat or the fight-or-flight response, which can push the brain into a state of overarousal in a millisecond.

So in other words, low levels of arousal can cause the brain to become understimulated and bored. Ideal levels of arousal result in a perfect balance that supports an optimally attentive state in the performance zone. Too much stimulation pushes the brain into a state of overarousal, which easily translates into stress.

The tidal fluctuations between overarousal, underarousal and optimal arousal can be best illustrated by the arousal curve. *The arousal curve*, also known as the Yerkes-Dodson Law, was defined by a model developed in 1908, and it has withstood the test of time.

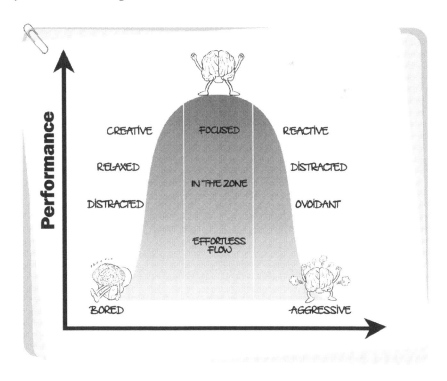

The Yerkes-Dodson law states that when arousal increases, so too does performance – but only to a certain critical point where the brain and body are in perfect alignment. Further arousal past that point only decreases performance, as demonstrated by the inverted U shape or "curve."

This depiction of the arousal curve illustrates that the left side of the curve is where the brain is relaxed. The right side of the curve is where the brain is more stressed. At the bottom of the left side, the brain is bored and unfocused. At the bottom of the right side, the brain is in distress and unfocused.

At the top of the curve, the brain is in "the zone" where it is perfectly tuned for optimal attention and performance. When we wake up in the morning, we start somewhere on this arousal curve. Some of us might be starting on the left in a relaxed but unfocused state, while others might be starting the day already on top of the curve, or even on the right (stressed), depending on the state of our physiology as well as our circumstances.

Let's say you wake up in the morning on the left side of the curve, which is the most common scenario. The brain tends to be less-focused and underaroused. That's one reason executives often go for that first cup of coffee in the morning, since coffee consumption increases levels of adrenaline and thus contributes to arousal.

Throughout the workday, numerous situations and interactions are likely going to push your brain up over to the right of the curve. As your brain hits the top of the curve, you're going to be focused for a little while.

But at some point, something might occur that results in an increase of hormones in the prefrontal cortex, which pushes the brain over the top and to the right side of the curve. This results in feelings of stress. Occurrences that cause this might include an overload of work, a problem with a co-worker, bad personal or company news, or even just an annoying email or phone call.

A brain that resides on the right side of the arousal curve is primed for fight or flight, and will therefore begin to focus on seeking out threats, even when threats are not present. This is when a person tends to make more out of an issue than is warranted, responding more dramatically than someone whose brain resides either on top of the curve or to the left of it.

On the other hand, when a brain is required to perform tasks it perceives as boring – such as sitting through a long-winded and uninteresting presentation – the brain may become underaroused and bored.

When the brain is bored, it tends to look for novelty and reward. The moment that the brain starts shifting to the left side of the curve, it's going to start seeking interesting things to focus on. You can tell when people are underaroused because they start looking at their watches or mobile phones.

So when the brain is on the left side of the curve, it seeks novelty and reward as its distraction, and when it resides on the right side of the curve, it seeks threat, which also becomes a distraction. Therefore, only when the brain resides at the top of the curve is it able to resist all temptation and maintain voluntary attention on the task at hand.

Clearly, the longer we can keep the brain at the top of the arousal curve, the more we will get done in a day. And the longer we can keep our employees' brains in that optimal zone, the more productive the whole company will be.

Temptation and Performance

Even though the brain is easily distracted when it resides on either side of the arousal curve, that doesn't mean we don't have the capacity to resist the temptation of distraction. The brain's ability to resist temptation has interested psychologists for decades, and it's an area that's been heavily studied.

One of the most referenced studies on our ability to resist temptation is known as "The Marshmallow Study," which was conducted by Stanford University in 1967. In it, 1,000 children were presented with a marshmallow and told that they would be left alone, unsupervised, for 20 minutes. They were told that if the marshmallow was still there when the researcher returned, they would actually receive two more marshmallows. In other words, they would be rewarded for exercising some self-control.

About 30 percent of those kids responded like I would have – they ate the marshmallow right away. Another 30 percent played around with the marshmallow for a while, but eventually ended up eating it.

Roughly a third, however, were able to override the impulse to immediately eat that marshmallow. They knew there was going to be a bigger reward if they could hold out and delay their gratification, and they were able to do it. This is what we call *impulse inhibition.*

What's particularly fascinating and useful about this study is that these children have been followed for almost 50 years. And as it turns out, the children who showed an ability to inhibit their responses during the study consistently demonstrated the best academic performance in school and achieved the most success in life. Interestingly, they also turned out to be the healthiest.

One might argue that impulse inhibition is a genetic gift, and that these children were born with the brain capacity to inhibit impulsive behavior. This may be true to some extent. But some children are born with athletic talent, and those children do not necessarily become elite athletes. Conversely, less-talented kids sometimes become top-level athletes.

It's true that there are individual differences in our "machinery" that enables us to remain attentive and avoid distractions. In some of us, that mechanism works extremely well; in others, it may not be as strong. But the good news is that whatever the innate capacity of our given "instrument," it can be developed and strengthened.

With sustained attention being such an important skill for performance, one might be inclined to assume that the part of the brain involved in impulse control would take up a large portion of the prefrontal cortex. Unfortunately, this is not the case. The areas of the brain involved in impulse control are in fact so small that their exact locations eluded scientists for decades.

Thanks to advances in neuroimaging technology, we are now beginning to learn where these self-control centers are located. These centers go by fascinating names such as the *medial-prefrontal cortex*, the *orbitofrontal cortex*, the *right-ventrolateral-prefrontal* cortex and the *dorsolateral prefrontal cortex* – all of which refer to the anatomical location within the prefrontal cortex.

These self-control centers consist of clusters of neurons that project into the limbic areas of the brain to exert some control over our impulses. As you might recall, our impulses are directed by the limbic brain, which has a complete disregard for long-term consequences of our behaviors – often getting us into more trouble than getting us out of it.

We are now learning that the strength of these neuronal projections determines our effectiveness in maintaining self-control. This discovery has provided insight into the mental condition Attention Deficit Hyperactivity Disorder, or ADHD, which is partly characterized by inattention and impulsive behavior.

In a 2009 article in the journal Brain Mapping, researchers examined the brains of people with ADHD and discovered that people with ADHD have fewer connections between the neurons in the self-control centers, than people without ADHD. This fact potentially renders those self-control areas as less effective in overriding impulsive behaviors in people with ADHD.

Consider all this in the context of the average work environment. On an average workday, the self-control centers work overtime to resist all manner of temptations and distractions, and inhibit all kinds of impulses.

We may stop ourselves from yelling at irritating co-workers, acting out at a clumsy intern, or refusing to listen to an impatient client who is calling for the hundredth time. We may resist the temptation to eat all of those yummy cookies in the pantry, to check social media or go online shopping when we're writing a proposal, and to look at our phones when we're in a boring presentation.

Over time, these self-control centers become fatigued, resulting in a decreased capacity to inhibit impulses. At some point, the self-control centers become so exhausted they simply go offline, leaving our brains at the mercy of our limbic systems.

Depending on where we are at that moment on the arousal curve, the limbic brain will either seek reward or seek threat. At that point, irritating co-workers, interns and clients better watch out; and oh yes, those cookies are all ours. And we will not only check our phones during that boring presentation, we'll play a few games while we're at it.

The good news is, there's an upside. In a groundbreaking study in 2010, researchers from Queen's University in Canada trained rats in the art of self-control and observed their brains in the process. The researchers observed that with the practice of inhibiting impulsive behaviors, the self-control centers in the brain grew stronger by developing stronger connections between neurons.

What this teaches us is that being born with weaker self-control centers does not automatically dictate a life sentence of distracted behavior, poor impulse control and poor attention. Nor does the wearing nature of relentless workplace exhaustion have to render us helpless at some point in the day.

Instead, with adequate amounts of training, any one of us can build those self-control centers at will, just like we build our muscles when we exercise.

Chapter Seven

Strategies to Improve
Sustained Attention

"Lack of direction, not lack of time, is the problem.
We all have 24-hour days."
Zig Ziglar

As you can see from the previous chapter, our physiology plays a large role in where we stand on the arousal curve, and the self-control centers' stamina is key to our ability to sustain attention and inhibit impulsive behavior. Extensive research has shown that physical exercise and nutrition have a strong effect on both of these elements.

Earlier, I mentioned that the performance zone between underarousal and overarousal is like a "Goldilocks" zone, where the cocktail of neurotransmitters and hormones needs to be "just right." It goes without saying that both exercise and nutrition have a strong impact on our physiological status, making them strong influencers in our capacity to sustain attention and improve performance.

Exercise and Sustained Attention

In Chapter 4, I addressed the role that exercise plays in combating stress, which is to burn off those stress hormones. By re-establishing hormone balance in this way, exercise can shift brain arousal back toward the performance zone.

Interestingly, exercise not only decreases overarousal, but also *increases* arousal in the brain when it is underaroused. As we begin to exercise, tissues in our bodies and brains require greater amounts of oxygen and glucose. Also, hormones come into play – the same ones we usually want to keep in check to avoid overarousal.

Adrenaline is largely responsible for switching on the heart and lungs so they can increase their rate of work. Cortisol, too, has a role; it enables the release of glucose from the liver so it can be utilized as an energy source.

As adrenaline and cortisol levels rise in the body, they naturally rise in the brain. This also increases our ability to pay attention as we enter the performance zone on the arousal curve. Exercise, therefore, may be one of the most powerful tools for helping the executive to voluntarily remain in the performance zone.

Another benefit of exercise is the strengthening effect it has on the self-control centers in the prefrontal cortex. When we exercise at an intensity that makes us feel a bit uncomfortable, we are presented with an opportunity to either act on the impulse to stop or slow down – or we can override the impulse and keep ourselves going. By practicing this skill in an exercise setting, we are also strengthening the exact same self-control centers that are required in our day-to-day lives.

This was recently confirmed through a study by researchers at the University of Exeter and Cardiff University in the United Kingdom. In their study, they asked participants to practice self-control through physical movement, and then they later observed the participants' gambling behaviors. What they discovered was an immediate decrease in impulsive decision-making after physically practicing self-control.

Finally, it's worth mentioning the benefits of brief bouts of mindfulness meditation on our ability to inhibit impulsive behaviors. Mindfulness meditation is a simple form of meditation where participants practice sustained attention on their breathing, while simultaneously keeping the mind from "wandering off" and becoming involved in other thoughts.

In 2010, a team of researchers from the University of North Carolina at Charlotte compared a control group that relaxed by reading a book versus a research group that participated in four brief instruction sessions of mindfulness meditation. Participants from both groups underwent cognitive testing before and after the four sessions and the results were astonishing. Even though both groups *felt* more relaxed and happier, the mindfulness group improved *tenfold* in cognitive function and sustained attention compared to the control group.

It's a reasonable conclusion that while by themselves they offer tremendous benefits, exercise *and* meditation are an extremely powerful combination for cultivating impulse inhibition and attention.

Exercise Strategy to Improve Sustained Attention

Based on the research covered in the previous section, ideally we would want to engage in any form of exercise that makes us huff and puff a little, while simultaneously practicing mindfulness meditation.

Because combining physical exercise with a meditative practice is so powerful, exercise forms such as tai chi and yoga are excellent ways to improve levels of sustained attention. However, not everyone is interested in taking up these types of exercise.

One of the greatest disadvantages of these forms of exercise is that for most people, enjoying the full benefits does require a degree of expert instruction. For the average executive, dedicating extra time to learning these forms of exercise and attending instructed classes may not be feasible.

In my years of coaching and working with executives, I've often encountered clients who simply did not have the time, courage or desire to learn yoga or tai chi, but who *were* prepared to engage in some form of physical activity on their own. For that reason, I developed a **sustained attention workout** that can be practiced while walking, running, swimming or climbing stairs. I like to call this workout *Exercise in 4 Dimensions*.

Over the past few years, quite a bit of research has been conducted on activities that concentrate and sustain attention. Many individuals still swear by classic long-endurance cyclical exercises such as running, cycling, swimming and walking.

These exercises are sometimes called *cyclical* because the limbs make the same cyclical movements over and over again. Cyclical movements stimulate the production of serotonin, a neurotransmitter in the brain that's well-known to act as a powerful antidepressant. High levels of serotonin can make us feel happy and calm, while low levels of serotonin can make us feel depressed, and can also promote impulsive behavior.

In a 2008 review in the journal, "Aggression and Behavior," the authors explain that serotonin modulates the impulsive effects of dopamine (another mood-regulating neurotransmitter) in the prefrontal cortex. Without a "braking" system, dopamine levels can soar, increasing the likelihood that the brain will seek distractions.

When excessive dopamine levels cause the brain to seek distractions, those distractions can take the form of rewards. But elevated dopamine can also cause the brain to seek threats, since a serotonin/dopamine imbalance can cause not only impulsive but also aggressive behavior. Serotonin, therefore, is a powerful mediator of impulsive behavior. And according to research, endurance exercise boosts serotonin production in the brain.

One catch-22 challenge with endurance-type activities is that, while we might choose this form of exercise to boost sustained attention, the fact is that sustaining our attention to exercise for a long period can be difficult! If we're already attention-challenged, an endurance activity can create a real gauntlet for the brain – especially for a brain that is accustomed to residing on either side of the arousal curve.

One strategy for training sustained attention during exercise is to provide the brain with an opportunity to shift into the performance zone at the top of the arousal curve – for just a short period of time – and then allow it some "recovery" time to be unfocused.

In exercise science, we train endurance athletes through interval training. In interval training, we have athletes exert themselves for a short period at a high intensity, followed by a recovery period in which the athletes slow down for a bit. This exertion/recovery cycle is repeated for a specified number of periods.

When we're training for sustained attention, we can follow the same principle. But in this case, our work interval is coupled with a sustained attention interval, and our recovery period also allows the brain to be unfocused.

The length of the work interval period depends on how long you can hold your focus. During your exercise, you're going to find your mind wandering off from time to time. That's okay. Because this is a sustained attention *training* exercise, challenge your focus and recognize the point where your mind begins to wander off. Figure out the length of that period of time, and set the interval period just out of reach of your sustained attention capacity.

Exercise in 4 Dimensions simply means that we will be walking, running or cycling while simultaneously paying attention to both our outside and inside worlds. The outside world is a three-dimensional world, and our inside world, inside our bodies and minds, adds a fourth dimension – hence an Exercise in 4 Dimensions.

Here is an example of what an Exercise Routine in 4 Dimensions could look like using a three-minute interval and a one-minute recovery period.

In this example, we will be walking, but remember that this type of routine can also be practiced using other forms of endurance exercise. If you are a more experienced athlete, you may want to match the focus interval with a hard, intense work interval, and make your recovery period a low-intensity period.

Here we go!

Start by finding a steady pace at which you feel you are working reasonably hard, but not too hard. You should be able to have enough air to talk in short sentences, but not enough air to recite an entire passage out of Shakespeare's Macbeth while walking.

Maintain this tempo for the entire walk while setting a timer for three-minute focus intervals with one minute of recovery in-between. This means that you will be walking and paying attention for three minutes, and then walking and allowing your mind to wander for just one minute.

This exercise/practice does not allow for music, as that can be too distracting. The timer will help you pull your mind back to attention and limit the mind-wandering. For each three-minute block, focus on using one of your senses only – starting with vision, then hearing, then smell, taste, touch and proprioception (sensing your body in movement). Finish off by using the entire symphony (all your senses).

Here's a little more detail on how to focus with each of the senses.

Vision: For the first three-minute block, focus on every object you walk by. Start by focusing on objects that are far away, and try to make out the most minute details. Then switch to objects nearby, also focusing on the intricate details.

Next, focus on the many colors you pass by and try to take in as much as you can. After three minutes, keep the pace of your walk steady, but just allow the mind to wander without aim or agenda for one minute of recovery.

Hearing: During your second three-minute block, focus on what you hear. Try to avoid going with the loudest and most obvious sounds, but rather focus your attention on more faint sounds such as the sound of the wind, the chirping of birds, children playing in the distance, and so on.

Try to determine where the sounds are coming from so that you hear sounds from all directions, especially behind you. This exercise greatly heightens awareness and is also an excellent exercise to strengthen spatial awareness.

Again, after three minutes, keep the pace of your walk steady for one more minute, but allow the mind to wander.

Smell: During your third three-minute block, focus on what you smell. Take in full deep breaths through the nose and try to take in every scent possible. Trees, plants, people cooking, exhaust fumes, laundry soap – anything goes. With every smell, try to take in the cocktail of different scents.

And again, after three minutes, take a minute of recovery where you let go of this focus and allow the mind to wander.

Taste: Taste can be a bit tricky, but one way to support this exercise is to take a single food item such as a raisin and keep it in your mouth for the whole three minutes. While you are walking, try to fully experience the various taste sensations as the raisin rolls over your tongue and travels through your mouth. Pay full attention to every single detail.

Every walk can be a different taste test with different items. I do recommend using healthy and fresh food items to taste-test and not manufactured, packaged ones; those tend to contain additives that can ruin a perfectly well-executed taste exercise. These additives may also desensitize the brain's receptiveness to the natural flavors of foods.

Once again, after three minutes, let go of the focus on sensation and allow the mind to wander for one minute of recovery.

Touch: During this three-minute block, try to feel how the wind brushes up against your skin, and how your clothing rubs up against your body. Feel how the breeze brushes through your hair and the sensation of the sun (or rain!) on your face. Feel the cool or warmth of the air and the feel of the ground beneath your feet.

After three minutes, again let go of the focus on these sensations and allow the mind to wander for one minute of recovery.

Proprioception (body sense): For many people, this is one of the most difficult focus exercises. Typically, our senses are directed outward and away from our bodies, so turning the attention inward can be a challenging experience.

Begin with focusing on how the air flows into your lungs while you take long deep breaths. Then, visualize the soles of your feet touching the ground and imagine each square inch of your foot making contact with the ground. Finally, focus hard on trying to feel your pulse as your heart is pumping blood through your body.

After three minutes, let go of all focus and simply allow the mind to wander freely for one minute of recovery.

The Full Symphony: In the final three-minute block, use all of your heightened senses together as a symphony – a full, elaborate and unique composition of yourself and the world around you. Try to take in as much of the internal *and* external environment as you can while you are walking. For many people who were successful during the first six blocks, this can be a deep sensory experience. A conscious awareness of all six heightened senses together opens a much larger door to experiencing our world, and is an excellent focus exercise.

And after three minutes, let go of this focus, and allow your mind to wander for your final minute of recovery.

Even though exercising in itself is a great strategy to improve brain health and capacity, by engaging the brain during the exercise, we're able to challenge the brain in the same way we challenge our muscles. Through purposeful and consistent practice during exercise, we can gradually improve the brain's capacity to remain attentive on one task at a time.

Besides during exercise, it's also important to consciously challenge our time in the performance zone in other aspects of our lives, such as during work. This expanded practice ensures that the neurons flexed during exercise, also learn to fire in other situations in our lives that do not involve exercise.

For example, when writing an email and the phone rings, allow the phone to go into voice mail and try to override the brain's temptation to shift its attention to the phone until you have completed writing the email. Simple little strategies like these will help solidify the connections between the neurons that were created while exercising in 4 Dimensions. These connections are necessary for sustained attention.

Nutrition and Sustained Attention

Most people today will acknowledge that what we eat has an immediate as well as long-term effect on our ability to pay attention. There are many popular everyday terms that describe what foods can do to our brains. *Carb coma, sugar crash, caffeine rush* and *chocolate high* are just a few examples.

Many of these are generally considered to be short-term, minimally damaging consequences of a pleasurable and possibly even stress-relieving experience. However, there are instances in which our food choices can greatly inhibit our ability to pay attention for sustained periods of time.

In a 2007 study at Southampton University in the United Kingdom, researchers explored whether or not food coloring and food additives in processed foods would exacerbate symptoms of ADHD in children aged 3 to 8. What the researchers discovered is that a number of artificial food colorings, as well as sodium benzoate, have a dramatic effect on our ability to pay attention.

Sodium benzoate is a commonly used preservative in acidic foods, such as soft drinks, fruit juices, jams, jellies, sour candies and salad dressings. Artificial food coloring is in the vast majority of conventional packaged foods. The more vibrant the color, the more artificial colors it's likely to contain.

What these researchers also discovered is that we may all have varying levels of food sensitivities. In some of us the effects are so minor that we don't notice them, but in other people, those same foods could result in a serious, allergy-like response that raises histamine levels in the brain. Histamine, which is commonly associated with allergies, does not only have an effect in the body, but is also a powerful arousal agent in the brain. This is why people tend to feel drowsy when they take an antihistamine in response to allergies or during a common cold.

This shows that our food choices may have a direct effect on our arousal levels. What we choose for breakfast, lunch, dinner and everything in-between, could be influencing the brain's arousal level. For the executive who wishes to maximize time in the performance zone, choosing the right foods is essential.

Next, we will take a look at what foods can help maximize time in the performance zone and minimize time in the right or left sides of the arousal curve.

Nutritional Strategies to Improve Sustained Attention

The link between food and sustained attention simply lies in getting enough of the "right stuff" found in the right foods and avoiding, to your best ability, those foods that can be detrimental to your attention.

The typical human diet in today's first-world cultures tends to include a lot of processed foods that were manufactured for human consumption. Many of these foods contain chemicals and additives that could be detrimental to the brain's control centers as we saw in the previous chapter. Some foods can be quite harmless to some of us, but more harmful to others who have sensitivities to them. Some of these foods may also have very little nutritional value, which can limit the brain's capacity to remain attentive.

Furthermore, the poor nutritional quality of these foods often leads to the consumption of empty calories, which in turn contributes to weight gain. Weight gain, in itself, can have further negative effects on mood, self-esteem and sustained attention.

Avoiding consumption of processed foods and replacing them with high-quality, nutritious foods – such as **organic fruits**, **vegetables**, **nuts** and **seeds** – will help ensure the control centers in the brain remain switched on and active.

Specific nutrients in the diet can also be highly supportive for improved focus and sustained attention. Some key nutrients essential for the control centers in the brain are omega-3 fatty acids, the B vitamins, calcium, potassium and the amino acid tryptophan.

Omega-3 fatty acids, typically found in **coldwater fish** such as **salmon** and **mackerel** – as well as **nuts, seeds** and **avocados** – are essential fatty acids for the brain. In a 2010 article in "Life Extension Magazine," Dr. Julius Goepp explains that omega-3 fatty acids provide a large number of benefits for the brain, acting as a powerful antidepressant, anti-inflammatory and neuroprotective agent. In particular, omega-3 consumption improves connectivity between neurons.

As discussed earlier, the areas in the brain responsible for improving attention tend to have weaker connectivity in people suffering from attention deficit disorder. It's therefore plausible that omega-3 consumption and supplementation may benefit people suffering from attention deficit. Research in this area is beginning to show promising results in long-term consumption of omega-3 fatty acids and improvement in attention.

One of my mentors, Dr. Roy Sugarman, is a clinical neuropsychologist with more than 30 years of experience treating patients with anything from ADHD to depression, traumatic brain trauma to improving mental performance in world-class athletes. Dr. Sugarman is one of those visionary doctors who will only prescribe medication as a last resort and prefers to prescribe diet and exercise in his treatments before prescribing medication, where possible.

In a recent conversation over a morning cup of coffee, we talked about our favorite subject, neuroscience and health. He mentioned to me that his first "drugs" of choice that he prescribes to many of his patients are omega-3 fish oils. According to him, he has personally seen amazing results in some of his patients. However, he disclosed that the amount of omega-3 a person consumes, for any clinical condition, should be prescribed by a physician rather than through self-medication of over-the-counter products, since dosages can vary greatly per condition and patient.

Outside of a clinical application, omega-3 fatty acids are essential in our diets. Ensuring we are consuming sufficient amounts will not only help us improve our attention, but also protect the brain against age-related cognitive decline. They have even been shown to fully reverse age-related degeneration in the brain, says Dr. Kazuhiro Tanaka in his 2012 review of omega-3 and neuron function.

Several of the B vitamins, such as B-6 and B-12, are involved in the brain's energy production. The B vitamins niacin and folate have been shown to elevate mood. These vitamins are conveniently available in many whole foods, including **wheat**, **oats**, **beans**, **lentils** and **sweet potatoes**.

Calcium is most popularly known for its role in bone health, but it's also essential for effective communication between neurons. Both calcium and potassium function as conductors for the electrical charges that enable nerve impulses to travel from brain region to brain region. Without a constant supply of these nutrients, the neurons in the brain's self-control centers quickly lose their firing power.

The previous section briefly covered the relationship between exercise and serotonin in the brain. Tryptophan is an amino acid required for the manufacture of serotonin.

Research has shown that consuming high-protein foods such as turkey meat, while often touted as a tryptophan-rich solution, is actually an ineffective way to provide the brain with tryptophan. Because tryptophan is deemed nonessential by the body, the body will favor the more essential amino acids in the protein-rich food source, thus preventing tryptophan from entering the brain.

However, foods that are lower in protein but high in tryptophan – such as **kale**, **avocados** and **chickpeas** – stand a greater chance of providing the brain with tryptophan.

Another food source that has been proven to raise serotonin in the brain is **dairy**. If you choose to consume dairy, make sure you are tolerant to lactose and choose organically produced dairy from free-roaming cows that enjoyed a staple diet of meadow grass – not dairy from factory farm or feedlot cows. Those cows generally have been subjected to antibiotics, steroids and/or recombinant bovine growth hormone (rBGH), and live on a corn-based diet. There's scientific evidence that these drugs are present in the cow's milk, and can cause health issues in humans. Additionally, their use increases antibiotic resistance.

Cows that are fed grass and frolic happily in the meadows tend to produce higher-quality **milk** with higher levels of tryptophan.

Another food that appears to improve sustained attention is **peppermint tea**. Research shows that peppermint has properties that offer protection against the development of Alzheimer's disease, and help improve cognitive function.

One cup of **organically produced coffee** has also been shown to improve mental alertness and even short-term memory. If you choose to consume coffee, be aware that adding milk and sugar to your coffee adds to your calorie intake, which could be the tipping point in your daily caloric allowance. Also, consuming more coffee than the daily one-cup allowance can lead to overstimulation of your nervous system, pushing your brain to the right side of the arousal curve.

Foods that contain the amino acids lysine and arginine may also warrant some extra attention, as these amino acids have been shown to improve attention and decrease anxiety. **Greek yogurt,** which is also packed with probiotics, is an excellent source of lysine and so are **eggs, broccoli, lentils, bananas** and **peaches.**

Arginine contains nitric acid, which has been shown to relax blood vessels and lower blood pressure, thus improving blood circulation in the brain as well. **Oats** and **quinoa** are excellent sources of arginine, as are **walnuts** and **pumpkin seeds.**

Chapter Eight

Jennifer: A Case Study in Sustained Attention

"Focus more on your desire than on your doubt, and the dream will take care of itself. You may be surprised at how easily this happens. Your doubts are not as powerful as your desires, unless you make them so."

Marcia Wieder

Jennifer is an IT team leader for a major financial company. She is analytical, knowledgeable and possesses great people skills.

She is single and without children, so Jennifer has been able to pour all her energy into her work. In a reasonably short period of time, she has climbed the corporate ladder to a senior leadership role stationed in Hong Kong. Her rapid career growth has inadvertently placed her into a group of peers with much more work experience than her.

Jennifer takes pride in her reputation as a "can-do" person who always gets the job done. As a result of this reputation, the head office in New York assigned Jennifer an additional new function, which requires her to approve all transactions that occur in her branch.

This added challenge caused some tension, hostility and gossip in her office, as many of the senior executives did not respect her newly appointed position of authority. The gossiping and resistance from her colleagues began adding pressure to an already heavy workload.

Jennifer found herself trying to multitask between dealing with hostile colleagues, auditing transactions and completing her original workload. She tried to meet this challenge head-on by going to work earlier and leaving later, and she began to take work home with her regularly. At one time she had enjoyed managing her growing collection of duties as a sign of her competence and status, but with this increased pressure she began to feel exhausted all the time and found it a struggle to get things done.

When Jennifer finally left work late at night, she found comfort in eating high-fat foods in lavish restaurants, and enjoying a bottle of wine with her dinner. As a result, over the past year, Jennifer gained a lot of weight and found herself feeling physically exhausted, even from something as simple as walking from the subway stop to her office.

Jennifer initially called me to help her manage her energy and her weight. She was growing extremely tired of feeling exhausted all the time. During our first session, of course one of the first things we discussed was nutrition and exercise. At first, I met with some resistance on these topics.

Looking at her workload and long work hours, Jennifer simply could not see how she could squeeze in any exercise. She was also reluctant to give up her habit of eating out at night, as she felt it was the only thing that made her happy.

According to Jennifer, this "reward" was the one thing she had to look forward to during the workday. Often the thought of a nice dinner and bottle of wine was all she needed to find the extra motivation to keep going at work.

Simply the *thought* of exercise and the topic of nutrition was enough to shift Jennifer's brain in a state of overarousal. With her brain on the right side of the arousal curve, she immediately began to focus more on the problem than on the solution.

To pull her brain back into the performance zone of the arousal curve, I redirected the conversation to one about managing her energy at work. I asked Jennifer to tell me what a common workday looks like for her. I wanted to know her daily objectives, a general timeline and her accomplishments in a typical day.

167

As an example, she recalled a day earlier in the week when she had to write a thousand-word report on the status of her audits. Compounding the deadline were two additional scheduled meetings. Jennifer's description also revealed that she had scores of emails to attend to, as well as staff walking in and out of her office taking up a lot of her time and energy.

Her workday typically started off with checking and answering emails for about 30 minutes to one hour. I asked her if she spent the whole hour focused on the emails, or if there were occasional distractions. She confessed that, while she was checking emails, she would also be receiving texts on her phone from friends and family. Further, she often opened Facebook in a different browser window to see what was happening with her friends and family.

As the morning progressed, Jennifer tried to start working on her report, but as she did, the Facebook browser window remained open and she continued to check it. She also received text messages and had two conversations with employees about other matters.

At 10 a.m. she had her first meeting, which took around 90 minutes, after which she tried to get back to her report. She managed to finish her report by skipping lunch, which got her to the 2 p.m. meeting. That meeting took approximately an hour. At around 3 p.m. she headed back to her emails, but first stopped by the pantry for a snack as she often did because, by that time, she was starving and feeling exhausted.

Her typical quick snack would be any cookies or cakes she could get her hands on, along with a cup of coffee doctored with full-fat cream and sugar. She then hoped to get some of her auditing work done. This required writing a number of emails, along with follow-up phone calls. After sending five emails asking for data, she would start receiving responses from colleagues that required her attention.

This was a part of her job she found particularly exhausting. Her colleagues often questioned why she needed the data rather than simply giving it to her, or would come up with excuses delaying the data.

By that time of the day, Jennifer was short on patience for dealing with all of this, making her emails short and authoritative in tone. Some colleagues responded well to this, but others sent even nastier emails back, or just stopped answering altogether.

This tended to go on for hours. By the time everyone was heading home, Jennifer was still trying to compile the necessary data for her audit. Utterly exhausted, she left the office late at night feeling unaccomplished. The anxiety about not finishing her work compounded the fatigue, driving her to seek out a quiet restaurant to enjoy a nice meal and a bottle of wine before heading home.

Jennifer's Behavioral Strategy:

Jennifer's timeline showed a number of energy-depriving markers, such as the Facebook browser window, operating her computer and mobile phone simultaneously, skipping lunch and allowing unscheduled conversations and emotionally draining email conversations.

After bringing this to her attention, we agreed to restructure her priorities and to focus on expanding her sustained attention capacity so that she was not rapidly jumping from one task to another. She agreed to start by working only one communication device at a time. If she were working on the computer, she would switch off her phone, and vice versa. Also, opening multiple browser windows on the computer was draining her attention capacity, so she also decided to use only one browser window at a time to limit the temptation of seeking novelty on Facebook.

Furthermore, Jennifer learned how to identify her brain's state of arousal by imagining a speedometer on her forehead with a needle indicating the level of arousal. If Jennifer was feeling underaroused and started seeking novelty, such as Facebook, she would stop herself from jumping to the novelty item and imagine herself being really excited about completing her work task. She also needed to identify when her brain was overaroused, as would happen during her afternoon email conversations with colleagues she perceived as uncooperative.

In those moments where she felt frustrated or angry, Jennifer learned that she could refrain from sending out more emails and instead spend a few minutes shifting her arousal to the left into the performance zone. She would do this by focusing on deep breathing and paying attention to her immediate external and internal environment.

This would help her quiet the angry dialogue going on in her head. And refraining from sending more emails would meanwhile keep the situation from escalating in ways that would cause further irritation. Finally, Jennifer agreed to try single-tasking rather than multitasking. This included allocating planned "social time" with colleagues so as to minimize the amount of time in which colleagues wandered into her office and disrupted her concentration.

Jennifer's Exercise Strategy:

Because Jennifer felt anxious about dedicating some of her limited time to exercise, we agreed that she would wear a pedometer in the office that tracked the number of steps she took during the day.

During her first week, the number of steps she recorded was very low at only 1,500 steps per day. With this baseline number set, we then discussed a strategy to increase her number of steps each week. Jennifer felt that increasing her number of steps by 500 steps per week, or 100 steps per workday, was achievable.

Jennifer also agreed to go for a lunchtime walk each day, during which she would practice the sustained attention exercises described in the previous chapter – starting with one-minute sets of attention practice followed by one-minute periods of relaxed inattention. Each week, she would increase the duration of attention by 30 seconds.

Jennifer's Nutrition Strategy:

One of Jennifer's challenges was that she didn't wake up hungry, so she never ate breakfast. Further, more often than not she was too busy to eat lunch. As we discussed Jennifer's nutrition, it became clear to her that she needed to fuel her brain by eating more regularly, so she agreed to include breakfast and lunch in spite of her challenges with these meals.

For breakfast, Jennifer would either have oatmeal or Greek yogurt with some berries. For lunch, she felt that it would be easier to bring food in to work and eat at her desk, so she could use the full lunch break to go for her walk. Her lunch would either be a salad or a whole-wheat sandwich including a good source of omega-3 fats, such as avocado or salmon.

Jennifer also agreed to bring in an afternoon snack, such as raw almonds or a piece of fruit, to help fuel her brain during those afternoon hours. Initially, she was very reluctant to make any changes in her dinner or her alcohol use, so we simply agreed that she would try her best to choose healthier options at that meal only if she wanted to. For now, we would focus on breakfast, lunch and snacks to make the biggest difference.

Jennifer's Results

At first, implementing changes into her lifestyle was a challenge for Jennifer. For the first week or two, she would often find herself falling back into old habits. But during our coaching sessions, Jennifer learned to focus her attention on the small victories, and allowed herself to feel grateful for every accomplishment.

She did discover that exercising was much easier than she thought it would be, and this in itself was a great accomplishment for her. She particularly enjoyed the focused attention during her afternoon walks, which had a calming effect.

As weeks went by and Jennifer increased her number of steps per day, she began to feel more in control of her workday. She found herself looking forward to her energizing afternoon walks more than she looked forward to her late-night dinners, which she came to realize were only making her feel more tired.

After one month, Jennifer was walking 6,000 steps per day and was much more diligent with her food and water intake. The calmness and sense of self-control she felt in the afternoons as a result really helped her in her communications with her colleagues.

Jennifer discovered that this calmness had an interesting effect: her colleagues seemed much more compliant with her requests for data. She realized that in the past, her colleagues probably responded to her exhausted, overaroused brain (and resulting terse emails) by being more resistant to her communications. Once she became calmer and more relaxed, so did her colleagues. This greatly improved the effectiveness of her audits.

After two months, Jennifer disclosed that she hadn't been going out for as many late dinners, and she had stopped drinking so much wine. She admitted that she realized eating heavy meals and drinking so much alcohol at night really affected her performance the next day.

Another pleasant side effect of all this was that Jennifer started to notice some weight loss, even though she didn't feel like she was really trying to lose weight. This result further inspired Jennifer to join a local gym with a few of her friends, where they enjoyed taking dance fitness classes.

After six months, Jennifer was a person transformed. Her levels of energy had soared, and she was getting tons of work done in much less time, leaving more time to have fun with her friends and to exercise. What's more, she had developed a reputation at work as someone who didn't just get the job done, but who always had time and patience to coach others in getting *their* work done.

Through nutrition, exercise and brain-training, not only did Jennifer transform her health and her performance as an executive – she blossomed into a valuable leader. This was acknowledged at her next performance appraisal, which resulted in a much-deserved promotion.

Chapter Nine

Creativity and Performance

"I never made one of my discoveries through the process of rational thinking."
Albert Einstein

I have a confession to make. This being my first book, I discovered early in the process that I broke a cardinal rule in book writing.

After I came up with the idea to write this book, I simply went ahead and started writing it. I completed the first draft in just a few months, as the ideas seemed to flow from my head into the computer with relative ease.

After I was done with the first draft, I found myself with a manuscript that didn't have a working title. It wasn't until my editor asked me for a working title and an idea for the cover that I started to give it some thought. I later learned from a number of fellow authors that they envision the cover and working title long before they start writing the book, and thus write the book to match the cover and title.

This put me at a bit of a disadvantage, because I was now left with the arduous task of imagining a working title and cover that could match the content, and not the other way around.

For months, I tried to stretch the limits of my imagination, only to come up empty-handed. Not once did I experience writer's block during the writing of my book – but coming up with a working title and idea for a cover felt like a nightmare.

It seemed, for some reason, that my creativity was limited to the written word only. Turning my words into images was just not something my brain seemed willing to do. Every time I paused to explore my imagination and try to come up with a working title, I drew a blank. It was like staring into an abyss from which nothing was emerging.

I consulted my friends, my wife, a writing coach and even professional designers to help me develop an idea, but nothing seemed to work. I knew that the cover and title needed to represent the contents of this book, and that they needed to illustrate the link between our health and brain function. But no matter how hard I tried, no concept seemed to work properly.

Often, I would become frustrated at what felt like my own incompetence to think of something that should be easy. Until something magical happened.

The moment the idea came to me was so profound, I can remember exactly how it happened. I had just finished a very busy week at work and spent Saturday working on my book. By the time Saturday evening rolled around, I was exhausted. I decided to get a good night's sleep and was unconscious by 9:30 p.m.

I woke up at the crack of dawn on Sunday morning and found myself in a very quiet house, as the rest of the family was still asleep. I decided to make use of my time by going for a relaxed jog. I put on my running shoes and stepped outside to witness one of the most gorgeous sunrises I have experienced in a long time. The sun was just coming up over the horizon, and the sky was bright orange, with beams of sunlight bouncing off white clouds floating in the sky. Nature was putting on a light show. The air was nice and cool, but not too cold.

I left my house at a slow jog and made my way on my usual route to a golf course located nearby. As I ran through the golf course, the green grass smelled like it was freshly mowed. In the distance, a white mist was leaving the grass as the morning dew evaporated and its vapor was rising to meet the clouds up in the sky.

The weather was amazing, the scenery stunning, and I felt light on my feet as if I could keep going forever. The path through the golf course eventually took me to a large reservoir, which had been converted into a nature preserve. Surrounded by trees and water, I kept going. While I was taking in my environment, my mind began to wander. I was enjoying my run so much, and I was in such a relaxed state, it was almost as if I was in a trance.

That's when it hit me. It came out of the blue without any announcement whatsoever. The book cover flashed before my eyes with the title, "Headstrong Performance." As clear as day, I could see the image before me. I had just experienced my very own "eureka" moment.

Following that visualization of my book cover, my brain experienced a tsunami of energy and excitement. It was so intense and electrifying, it actually stopped me dead in my tracks. Immediately, I turned around and sprinted back home, where I grabbed a notebook and began sketching out my idea. The idea eventually became the official cover and title of this book, with the help of a graphic artist.

What I experienced on that Sunday morning is referred to in neuroscience as *insight*, which is where the creative process tends to begin. As I learned through direct experience, insight can't be forced. Unlike sustained attention, which in a way can be willed by managing our levels of arousal in the brain, the "aha!" moment seems to be something that only presents itself when the brain is ready and willing to reveal it.

The interesting thing about insight is that it tends to happen when the brain is actually *unfocused* and not really paying attention to anything. It's almost averse to sustained attention.

In today's average working environment, where the executive's brain is shifting rapidly from one end of the arousal curve to the other, the brain rarely has time to be unfocused. This makes creativity in the workplace appear to be a rare phenomenon, available only to a select few who seem to access it more readily than the rest of us.

But in reality, the capacity for creativity is not something that is limited to those who possess a talent for it. It is accessible to all professionals under the right conditions.

Creativity in the Workplace

Creativity is the tendency to generate or recognize ideas, alternatives or possibilities that may be useful in solving problems, communicating with people or entertaining ourselves and others.

Creativity is therefore not the sole domain of professionals in overtly "creative" professions or industries. All employees encounter moments in their jobs when they need to solve problems or generate ideas.

Research on creativity in the workplace shows that companies that invest in fostering creativity actually drive market share, increase financial returns, improve consistently and have greater customer satisfaction compared to those that don't.

Creativity is thus a viable and necessary generator of revenue for organizations and executives looking to get ahead in their industries.

According to a 2010 article in Bloomberg Businessweek, IBM surveyed 1,500 CEOs and asked, "What is the most important thing you want out of your executives?" The leaders identified *creativity* as the most important leadership competency for the successful enterprise of the future. They recognized that today's business model has evolved, and that to stay ahead of the game, their companies needed to innovate.

As I mentioned earlier, creativity is such a challenging phenomenon because it can't be forced at will. It can only be harvested under the right conditions. This means that in order to develop a creative culture of executives, we need to create an environment that fosters creativity.

Besides an unfocused mind, key ingredients for creativity appear to be happiness and gratitude. The creative experience that I encountered during my jog is a good example. I started the jog in a state of profound appreciation for the environment around me.

Neuroscience is also teaching us that happy people can access the creative areas of their brains more than unhappy people. Author and researcher Shawn Achor wrote in his book, "The Happiness Advantage," that when employees are happy – creativity, resilience, motivation and productivity rise significantly.

As we discussed earlier in this book, healthy employees tend to be the happiest ones, making exercise and nutrition very important components in the cultivation of creativity.

Insight and Performance

From an evolutionary perspective, our capacity for creativity has enabled us to effectively adapt to and even master our environment. This is a key factor in our success as a surviving and thriving species. Evolution is one huge creative exercise. Think about the initial use of fire and how that changed life on earth, or the development of tools that led us to the invention of the wheel.

A few years back, I watched a movie called "Cast Away," in which the character Chuck Noland (played by Tom Hanks) survives a plane crash and finds himself alone on a remote island. On this island, he is forced to learn basic survival skills, such as foraging, hunting, creating shelter and making fire. Chuck quickly learns how city life has ill-prepared him to survive in the wild, and that nature is a relentless teacher. But in time, he not only learns how to survive, but develops and masters the skills required to thrive.

In one scene, Chuck knows he will need to create fire, so he sets out trying to do this with some branches, leaves and two stones that he rubs together to create sparks. Unfortunately, he can't get a fire going.

Numerous items have landed with him on the island. One is a volleyball that has the name of the manufacturer – Wilson – on it. Chuck starts talking to the volleyball as "Wilson," in effect befriending it. Wilson eventually becomes Chuck's companion and a major "character" in the movie.

After a full night and day of trying and repeatedly failing to create a fire, Chuck's frustration rises as his brain's levels of arousal shift too far to the right. Eventually, the frustration and fatigue become too much for his brain to process, and he finally loses it when a branch breaks and cuts his hand. Like the branch, he snaps, and he throws a tremendous tantrum.

With his bloodied hand, he grabs Wilson the volleyball and throws it against a tree, leaving a bloodstain on the ball that resembles a head with spiky hair. Some time after retrieving the ball and settling down, Chuck holds the ball in his hands and decides to draw eyes, a nose and a smile on the bloodstain, creating a smiley face that gives Wilson a more human look.

This seemingly unfocused "not-on-task" activity enables Chuck to shift his brain back to the left on the arousal curve. As he becomes calm, he has stopped paying attention to the problem for a moment, and has achieved a state of simply being present.

Chuck then strikes up a conversation with Wilson about the process of making fire – and it occurs to him in a dramatic "aha" moment, that what's needed to make fire is the special ingredient *air*. He then goes back to his task of making fire, but improves the circulation of air in the process. This enables him to successfully start a fire, and a wild celebration with Wilson erupts.

After several years on the island, he eventually develops the courage and the skills to build a raft and leave the island, which ultimately leads to his rescue.

The movie scenes of Chuck learning to start a fire illustrate four critical elements that were necessary for Chuck to access his creativity. First, Chuck unintentionally threw a massive tantrum, which was essentially a form of physical activity. Physical activity, even from a temper tantrum, burns off most of the excess stress hormones, such as adrenaline and cortisol. This allowed him to shift his state of arousal to the left on the arousal curve.

Second, when Chuck started to calm down, he engaged in a seemingly unrelated creative process: drawing a face onto Wilson. By doing so, he switched his focus away from the problem. Further, it turns out that the neural circuitry activated by drawing Wilson's face is the same neural circuitry involved in insight and creativity.

In a research paper published in the journal, "Psychonomic Bulletin & Review," researcher Arne Dietrich explains that voluntary creative activity – such as the act of drawing a face – involves a working relationship between many regions of the cerebral cortex. Those regions are the:

- Prefrontal cortex (located behind the forehead), which functions as the director of voluntary creativity;

- Hippocampus, which is involved in short-term memory;

- Motor cortex (located just behind the prefrontal cortex), which directs physical movements such as moving the hand, arm and eyes while drawing;

- Parietal cortex (located on top of the head just behind the motor cortex), which is involved in sensory stimulation; and

- Temporal lobes (located on the sides of the head near our ears), which are involved in long-term memory.

The act of drawing ignites and switches on the neural pathways between these regions of the brain, priming them for creativity.

Third, talking with Wilson was a social activity, and research shows that engaging in social activities raises levels of oxytocin in the brain. Oxytocin is perhaps best known as a hormone that mothers produce when breast-feeding, nurturing and hugging their children. Research also shows that oxytocin is produced by both men and women during many social bonding activities. Oxytocin has a calming effect on the brain, produces feelings of gratitude and happiness and acts as a powerful antidepressant and anti-stress aid.

This calming anti-stress effect, combined with Chuck's voluntary creative activity, allowed his brain to connect all the pieces of the creativity puzzle and create a single idea. This phenomenon is known as *spontaneous creativity*.

Spontaneous creativity seems to occur when the creativity stream travels in a reverse direction, from the subconscious brain into the conscious brain, the prefrontal cortex. As the prefrontal cortex is flooded with information from the subconscious brain, the sensation is much like a tsunami of information entering our consciousness. This flooding of information is why it feels "spontaneous."

Finally, when Chuck was ready, he re-engaged in his task – but this time he was able to direct his attention to finding a solution by shifting his brain into the performance zone on the arousal curve.

Now, let's translate that into a work setting. How many times do we struggle to solve a work problem and witness everyone around us becoming frustrated? Most of us see this happen nearly every day. And how often do we become so frustrated that everyone decides to ... get up and go bowling instead?

Never, right? That's because when the brain is focused on the problem, it tends to shift to the right on the arousal curve, and therefore treats the problem as a threat.

Like Chuck, most people who find themselves to the right of the arousal curve tend to get stuck there, getting more and more frustrated and moving further and further to the right of the curve – sometimes to the point of avoidance or aggression.

In that state of mind, doing something different is unlikely to occur to us, because in threat mode we become hyperfocused on the problem and can't see the forest, just the trees. Hyperfocus doesn't help creativity; actually, it's a killer of creativity.

As you might recall from the arousal curve discussion in Chapter 6, creativity is maximized when the brain is resting slightly to the left side of the arousal curve. By taking a step back and doing something different and/or social, even just for a short period of time, the brain is able to take a break and calm down so it can shift slightly to the left of the curve. This reinvigorates its capacity for insight and creativity. Once creativity is ignited, the excitement will drive the brain's level of arousal back into the performance zone, where it can sustain the required level of attention to get the job done.

A significant moment in real-life history where this phenomenon could have been observed is Einstein's development of the Theory of Relativity. As the story goes, one day Einstein was sitting under a tree watching shafts of sunlight filter through the clouds. To him, they looked like stairways to the heavens. As he relaxed, he mused about what it would be like to ride on a sunbeam.

I'm sure that if any of his peers had seen him at that moment, they would have interpreted Einstein as being a daydreamer and completely unproductive.

Yet it was during that bout of what looked like daydreaming that Einstein stumbled upon the insight that led to the Theory of Relativity. Once he had pondered the idea of traveling on light, he voluntarily shifted his brain into the performance zone and worked tirelessly and meticulously to scientifically compute how that could be done – thus revolutionizing how we look at space and time today.

Deliberate daydreaming might still be frowned upon in many work cultures, posing a bit of a challenge for the executive seeking access to creativity. However, there are ways to mask daydreaming activity so it looks more "productive" in the eyes of the layperson; we'll take a look at that potential in a moment. (With exercise and nutrition as a recurring theme, you might guess that they play a role.)

We can learn from the examples of Einstein and the "Cast Away" character Chuck – they show us that creativity is not limited to those who have some sort of special talent for it. It can be harnessed by any one of us.

We just need to exercise the awareness and courage to disengage when we find our brains shifting too far to the right of the arousal curve. We need to be willing to instead engage in a different activity, one that allows the brain to shift to the left on the arousal curve.

The reason this takes courage is that at times this shift may look like daydreaming, lack of focus, or even abandonment of the task – to our peers and superiors. Once the moment of insight hits, we then need to actively shift our brains back into gear – to the performance zone on the arousal curve – so we can turn the new idea or insight into a tangible product.

Chapter Ten

Strategies to Improve Creativity

"Physical fitness is not only one of the most important keys to a healthy body, it is the basis of dynamic and creative intellectual activity."

John F. Kennedy

Exercise and Creativity

Since the 1950s, researchers around the world have completed hundreds of studies assessing whether physical exercise has an effect on our creative capacity. Until recently, much of the research was inconclusive, and researchers wondered whether or not the increase in creativity was a secondary consequence of the mood improvement that comes with exercise.

Researchers have known for decades that exercise improves mood, and that a correlation exists between better moods and a greater capacity for creativity.

However, more recent research has shown that the effects of exercise on creativity are independent of mood, suggesting that physical exercise must evoke a positive response in the areas of the brain that are involved in creative thinking.

In a 2014 study conducted by Stanford University, researchers discovered that simply being on our feet, without necessarily moving, makes us significantly more creative. One explanation for this, the researchers suggest, is that when the brain takes part in semi-automatic processes that don't require too much of our attention – such as walking, driving a car or running – blood flow increases to the areas required for creativity.

The increased blood flow supplies those areas with oxygen and nutrients, thus priming them for creative thinking.

Another theory is that, compared with sitting, being on our feet requires much greater activity from the motor cortex. When standing, we need to activate many more muscles than when sitting down. There is also more activity in the sensory areas of the cerebral cortex, because standing involves constant monitoring of balance via pressure sensors in the feet and the middle ear. Standing, therefore, stimulates activity in the same neural networks involved in creativity, priming them further for creative capacity.

Furthermore, the motor cortex, which is involved in directing physical movement, seems to play a significant role in creativity. Research conducted on musicians shows that engaging in a highly creative process – like playing a musical instrument – improves creativity. Brain imaging studies on musicians have shown that when musicians simply *think* of playing their instruments, the brain activates the neurons in the motor cortex as well as in the arms and hands – in exactly the same way as if the musicians were playing the instruments for real.

This means that when we engage in physical activity, such as exercise, we may also be engaging the regions of the brain that are involved in creativity – just as when we play a musical instrument – thus priming them for creative capacity. This may be especially true when the physical activity has a creative component, such as with dance or moving in patterns.

Finally, research shows that physical play in groups can greatly improve creativity. For the most part, playing with other people creates bonding, which enhances the effects of the extra oxygen and nutrients and the stimulation of creative neural pathways.

Research conducted in 1964 by Marian Diamond and her colleagues shows that when rats live in a playful and stimulating environment, their brains actually grow and they become better problem-solvers. Since then, multiple studies have confirmed this effect in humans as well.

What we can learn from all this is that spending more time on our feet, as well as working in a playful environment with colleagues, stimulates our brains to such an extent that we can become smarter, more resourceful and more creative.

Exercise Strategies to Improve Creativity

In Chapter 7, I explained how endurance sports improve sustained attention. One reason for this is that serotonin, the neurotransmitter produced by endurance exercise, has dopamine-suppressive qualities. Suppressing dopamine helps improve sustained attention because elevated dopamine can cause the brain to seek distractions and threats and lead to impulsive behavior.

Yet while dopamine may not be the ideal neurotransmitter for sustained attention, it does seem to play a role in creativity. In her review published by the "Journal of Comparative Neurology," Dr. Alice Flaherty wrote that dopamine production is essential to creativity, because it has a role in idea-generation and novelty-seeking.

Serotonin-producing (endurance) activities may therefore be helpful for tasks that require long periods of attention. But apparently, when it comes to idea- generation and creativity, endurance activities may not be our best bet. However, other forms of exercise can produce favorable brain chemistry to support creativity.

One phenomenon we often hear endurance athletes talk about is the "runner's high" – a feeling of euphoria that occurs after a

192

period of intense physical exertion. A popular misconception is that this runner's high is caused by the production of endorphins, a group of morphine-like peptides that help us suppress pain.

Of course, producing our own morphine-like brain chemicals is a blessing in itself. This opiate system functions to suppress feelings of physical and emotional pain – whether dealing with an angry boss, a problem at work or aches and pains from a sport or race. But studies have revealed a more direct source of the runner's high.

Researchers from the Georgia Institute of Technology tested the neurobiology of undergraduate students running on a treadmill. To their amazement, they discovered that the runner's high stemming from prolonged exercise is actually caused by the production of another neurotransmitter – a class called endocannabinoids. These endocannabinoids are akin to a natural form of marijuana produced by the brain, and are responsible for those feelings of euphoria and happiness experienced during and after exercise.

Researchers recently discovered that smoking cannabis actually improved creativity in test subjects. Of course, this shouldn't mean that we start doping our executives with recreational drugs to improve creativity. However, what this does mean, is that the so-called runner's high may be a better alternative to ignite the creative spark within us – as long as we do not engage in activities that also increase the production of serotonin.

Physical play shows promise as a strategy to achieve just that balance – production of endocannabinoids without serotonin. Physical play has long been proven to boost social bonding, productivity, learning and creativity. The best forms of play are those that require physical exertion, occur in a social setting and evoke lots of laughter. Examples include team sports and tag games like laser tag or paintball.

These forms of physical play boost the dopamine that produces novelty-seeking oxytocin that removes anxiety, and endocannabinoids that provide a feeling of euphoria.

Another form of physical play that's catching researchers' attention for its creativity-cultivating potential is – perhaps surprisingly – video games. Researchers at Penn State University recently confirmed this potential by observing boosted creativity after playing the popular video game "Dance Dance Revolution" – a physical game where the player must follow the computer's dance steps.

Like many kids, my daughter has an Xbox 360 Kinect that tracks the movement of the player(s) and displays those movements in the game via an avatar. My daughter is an aspiring athlete, so her game choices tend to be related to sports and fitness, including dance, kickboxing and sports games.

While playing these games, my daughter and I actually break a sweat – and usually end up laughing at ourselves as we try to keep up with the games. Activities that evoke laughter have not only proven to improve scores on creativity tests in the lab, but also to boost productivity and employee engagement, says author Randall Munson in his book, "Serious Business of Humor!"

Finally, in 2012, researchers from the University of Utah and University of Kansas conducted an interesting field study in which they took 56 volunteers for a four-day hike in Alaska. Before-and-after tests showed a whopping 50 percent improvement in creativity scores. This study has since been duplicated using a three-hour hike. After three hours of hiking in nature, creativity levels increased by 20 percent.

So playing games, or even just hiking outdoors in nature, can greatly improve creativity.

One specific form of social, outdoor physical activity that has long been a popular pastime for many executives is the game of golf. In a recent article in "Forbes Magazine," the author notes that during a four-hour golf game, only six minutes are spent *actually playing the game of golf.* The rest of the time is spent walking and bonding with fellow players in a natural setting. The combination of nature, social bonding and physical exertion suggests that golf, so popular with executives, is indeed an ideal creativity-boosting activity.

Additionally, I described in the previous section how creativity is best cultivated on our feet. This too makes golf an ideal activity. The game includes all of the elements required to achieve the perfect cocktail of creativity-promoting hormones and neurotransmitters in the brain – providing, of course, that we walk the course and steer clear of driving golf carts.

Nutrition and Creativity

In 1851, Parisian artist Henri Murger wrote his classic book, "The Bohemians of the Latin Quarter." His novel consists of a series of interrelated episodes in the lives of a group of poor artists who try to maintain their artistic ideals while simultaneously struggling for food, shelter and other basic necessities.

His book spurred the popular notion that great artists must sacrifice a life of comfort to access unimaginable levels of creativity and artistry. The term "starving artist" soon became mainstream among aspiring artists, and the idea was unfortunately affirmed by Vincent van Gogh, who died poor.

Recent research in neuroscience, however, has dispelled the notion that access to creativity requires struggle and sacrifice. In fact, nothing could be further from the truth. To the contrary, creativity is best served by at least sufficient and adequate care and feeding of the brain and body.

As this chapter has already illustrated, an exhausting, frustrating struggle would naturally be counterproductive to the brain's capacity for creativity. Additionally, the idea that literally "starving" as an artist would improve creativity belies the connection between nutrition and brain function.

For one thing, since voluntary creativity requires an orchestrated collaboration between various brain regions that are directed by the prefrontal cortex, an adequate supply of glucose and oxygen needs to be constantly available to the brain.

Researchers in Scotland recently explored what happens to our brains when glucose levels drop too far. They showed that when glucose levels drop below a healthy balance, performance in the prefrontal cortex plummets considerably.

Interestingly, scores of research have also shown that when the brain has *too much* glucose, cognition declines as well. This means that the brain requires a delicate balance of glucose to function optimally and to access creativity. So even though being starved is *not* helpful for anyone who wishes to access a creative brain state, being overfed is equally destructive.

Recent research conducted by NASA confirms this. In their research of nutrition for astronauts, they discovered that poor glucose management also decreases psychomotor function, meaning the parts of the brain and nervous system that control movement. As discussed in the previous section, the motor cortex seems to be closely linked to creativity.

For the average astronaut, having poor motor function due to poor glucose balance could mean the difference between life and death for the entire crew.

For the average executive, the effects of poor glucose management might not be as dramatic, but in an increasingly competitive market, the slightest decrease in cognitive performance could mean the difference between being number one or ... number anything else.

A reasonably new discovery in this domain was first proposed by Dr. Mark Lyte in 1997. Dr. Lyte developed a theory that the bacteria in our intestines influence brain function immediately by signaling the brain through a neural pathway that he affectionately coined the "microbiome-gut-brain axis."

Initially, his theory was scrutinized by the scientific community, but after decades of persistence, Dr. Lyte is considered one of the greatest authorities in the now scientifically proven field of microbial endocrinology. In recent years, much research in this field has been conducted on both rats and humans, with some astonishing discoveries.

In a recent brain-imaging study conducted by researchers at UCLA, the brains of a group of women were observed before and after ingestion of probiotic bacteria-rich yogurt. Their brain function was compared to that of a similar group of women who ate yogurt without probiotic bacteria.

After four weeks, the women who consumed the probiotic-rich yogurt not only performed better in cognitive tasks, but also experienced better connectivity between neurons in the brain regions involved in a number of cognitive functions – including creativity.

If our intention is to support high levels of creativity through nutrition, then it's clearly vital that we consume adequate amounts of high-quality foods to sustain optimal glucose levels in the brain, and to improve the gut-brain axis.

Nutrition Strategies That Improve Creativity

In the previous chapter, I noted that balanced blood sugar is essential for brain function; without this balance, accessing the creative network in the brain is essentially impossible.

To achieve sufficient and sustained levels of blood sugar, the first vital strategy is to eat a healthy low-sugar breakfast.

Brain research has shown that the brains of individuals who don't eat breakfast actually respond much more drastically to the visual stimulus of junk food, thus increasing the likelihood that they will gravitate toward consuming high-sugar and high-fat foods, which in turn creates a glucose imbalance in the brain. Breakfasts that do the trick are meals that have undergone minimal processing and contain ingredients we can recognize from nature, such as **low-sugar fresh fruit with yogurt**, since yogurt also contains probiotics that improve creativity through the gut-brain axis. Some examples of low-sugar fruits are **apples**, **grapefruit** and all types of **berries**.

The second nutritional strategy for balanced blood sugar is to eat small portions and spread them out throughout the day, rather than just a few large heavy portions with long stretches in between.

Eating a big lunch and dinner with nothing in between will cause high blood-glucose levels in the brain after the meals – and then low blood sugar in the long periods without food. Instead, have a smaller lunch and dinner, with a low-sugar snack around mid-afternoon.

A simple strategy along these lines could be to eat half of a regular-size lunch and then take the other half to go, consuming the leftovers as your afternoon snack a few hours later. Another strategy could be to bring an afternoon snack in the form of an **apple** or other **low-sugar fruit**, and a handful of **almonds** or other **nuts**. A few other snack possibilities include a package of **whole-grain crackers** with a small piece of **cheese**, a few squares of **very dark chocolate** with a squeeze packet of **peanut butter**, a baggie of **carrots/celery/peppers** with a small container of **hummus**, or a **low-sugar energy bar** made of fruit and nuts without artificial ingredients.

Simple strategies like these can greatly improve blood-glucose levels, and provide the brain with the necessary fuel to access the neural networks involved in creativity.

Alcohol and Creativity

People have been consuming drugs and alcohol since the dawn of time. For thousands of years and across many cultures, various hallucinogenic plants and cocktails have been used by shamans and religious leaders to heal and gain access to "the gods." Even in the last few decades, our favorite rock stars and even secret government agencies have been known to experiment with hallucinogens in hopes of gaining deeper access to the creative networks of the brain.

Because we've all seen and heard so much about the potential connection between alcohol, drugs and creativity, I am often asked during my seminars and workshops about the effects of alcohol and whether it is a useful tool for accessing creativity.

Alcohol is quite commonly used by many individuals to "help them calm down" after a long and stressful day. For many people, moderate alcohol use may appear to be an effective strategy for relaxing and even for improving sleep.

Yet while some people do experience a calming effect, others experience exactly the opposite after consuming alcohol – finding themselves in a state of euphoria and excitement. For some, alcohol nullifies feelings of inhibition, making way for a night of partying and fun.

This apparent dichotomy makes the effect of alcohol on the brain fascinating to neuroscientists, and has baffled scientists for decades. Is alcohol a depressant or a stimulant?

Thanks to neuro-imaging studies, we're finally putting the pieces of the puzzle together. And the answer is both: it depends on which neurons are affected in the brain when we drink alcohol.

Research shows that our first drink stimulates the production of a neurotransmitter called GABA, one of a group of inhibitory neurotransmitters that suppresses neuron activity and calms the brain. Simultaneously, it inhibits the production of glutamate, which is an excitatory neurotransmitter in the brain. The increase in GABA and the decrease in glutamate result in a number of brain regions slowing and eventually shutting down.

The areas in the brain that shut down very quickly from the consumption of alcohol are the prefrontal cortex – the epicenter of consciousness, required for rational thinking, strategizing, impulse control and imagination – as well as the hippocampus, which you may recall is the center of memory processing.

In other words, the same mechanism that leads to the calm feeling from drinking alcohol shuts down the parts of the brain required for accessing creativity. While the prefrontal cortex and hippocampus essentially go to sleep, alcohol *is* also producing a stimulatory effect as it increases the production of norepinephrine and dopamine. This makes a person more excitable – and more motivated to repeat the behavior (drinking).

The areas of the brain that become excited are the subconscious regions and the limbic system, which is the epicenter of our "caveman instincts." It's no wonder, then, that after a few too many drinks some of us begin behaving like actual cavemen, with increasingly assertive and aggressive behavior.

In response to this, the adrenal glands begin to produce massive amounts of stress hormones, such as adrenal and cortisol. This creates a physiological response similar to the stress responses discussed earlier in this book.

Therefore, while we could be experiencing a *sensation* of calm and relaxation from a drink or two, we are actually setting the stage for a massive stress response in the body. Because the parts of the brain that would normally sense these effects are "switched off," we simply don't *feel* the effects of the stress on our bodies.

For this reason, alcohol is *not* a suitable tool to help us access creativity. It will actually create a shift to the right on the arousal curve. Chances are, after a long day at work, this is the last place we want the brain and body to go.

The best strategies for accessing creativity are really quite simple. Be physically active, go out in nature, play (including social time with others), laugh, drink lots of water, and eat small portions of healthy blood-sugar-regulating foods frequently (emphasizing whole, unprocessed, low-sugar, nutrient-dense foods with a balance of complex carbohydrates, proteins and healthy fats like omega-3s).

Not surprisingly, these simple strategies not only serve to make us more creative, but they are the same habits and practices proven to make us happier and healthier in every other respect. Happily, what works for the creative brain is really what works for health, longevity, stress management and focus.

Chapter Eleven

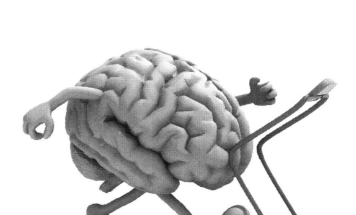

Mike: A Case Study in Creativity

"A dream is your creative vision for your life in the future. You must break out of your current comfort zone and become comfortable with the unfamiliar and the unknown."

Denis Waitley

Mike is the Creative Director of a large global advertising firm, and he's based in the company's Singapore office. He was stationed in Singapore four years ago as a promotion from his previous position in New York City.

Currently in his 50s, Mike just saw his last child graduate from New York University. He always imagined that once the children were out of the house, he would have more time with his wife Joanne, but when he came to see me, that had not happened yet – not even close.

During his past two decades with the firm, as the company grew, the number of projects with which he was involved grew exponentially. He was struggling to find balance between his demanding job and spending quality time with Joanne.

Mike also was concerned about his creativity. At one time, he took great pride in the fact that creative ideas would "just come to him," no matter how busy he was with work or with his family. Now that he was older, he felt as if it had become increasingly difficult to access his creative capacities at will.

Even though he was quite content with the creative performance of his team, he always enjoyed being able to outperform team members who were half his age. Yet he was reaching a point where younger team members seemed to outperform him creatively. The thought that one day he might not be able to add creative value scared him.

Finally, Mike was concerned because he also noticed that his memory was beginning to lapse, making it even more difficult to be organized at work. He contacted me with the hope that I could help him reinvigorate his creative capacity and sharpen his sense of clarity and memory.

During our initial conversation, Mike explained that being a Creative Director comes with too many additional responsibilities, which inhibit his ability to be creative.

Most days, Mike spends much of his time managing his staff, tracking their productivity and reporting back to the CEO and COO in New York. As he rises on the corporate ladder, he feels like the window of opportunity to be involved in creative processes is shrinking progressively.

Though he does enjoy his work responsibilities, he also likes to be able to roll up his sleeves and actively get involved with his team in the creative side of the work. However, due to his managerial workload, this has not happened in quite some time.

When I asked him about his relationship with exercise and eating a balanced diet, Mike told me that he was quite athletic when he was younger. In fact, he had been a triathlete in his youth and had even participated in the Kona Ironman – the most prestigious of all triathlons.

But later, work, family and life simply got in the way, as they do for so many people. Eventually he gave up triathlons and replaced them with the occasional walk or jog on the treadmill when he was on business trips. This activity slowly diminished further into a sedentary lifestyle.

His nutrition had also dropped in quality during this period. He often found himself skipping breakfast or lunch; snacking on doughnuts and potato chips at work; or grabbing hot dogs, burgers and fries on the way home from work. At home, he would then also eat the full meal that his wife cooked for him. After dinner, he and his wife would often sit and enjoy a bottle of wine together as he wound down from a stressful day.

These behaviors left Mike feeling exhausted almost all the time. Over the years, he also put on a considerable amount of weight, which he incorrectly attributed to the "natural" and inevitable effect of corporate life and aging.

Mike's Exercise Strategy for Creativity

Our first strategy to address Mike's concerns – the memory lapse, exhaustion, weight gain and most of all his lack of creative mojo – was to get him back into a regular exercise routine.

After explaining to Mike how exercising out in nature with other people has been shown to improve creativity, Mike decided to join his local triathlon group and start weekly triathlon training sessions.

Since endurance training by itself may not be as effective for stimulating creativity, Mike also decided to promote physical play with his team at work. He invested in a pingpong table and an interactive video system that included physical play games, to keep in the office. He encouraged playtime twice daily for himself and his team.

This strategy not only helped Mike, but his team members embraced it with great excitement and enthusiasm. The appreciation, loyalty and morale this move offered was a nice bonus in addition to the creativity that playtime generated.

Mike's Nutritional Strategy for Creativity

Mike agreed to start eating a healthy breakfast of yogurt and berries, and to bring along a piece of fruit to consume mid-morning in order to keep his blood sugar balanced.

He also agreed to make healthier choices for lunch. He decided to only eat half of his lunch at lunchtime and keep the other half for his mid-afternoon snack. By splitting his lunch in half, Mike would be able to keep his blood sugar levels even throughout the afternoon.

For dinner, Mike asked his wife to start cooking healthier, lighter meals, which she gladly did. If Mike got hungry before bedtime, he would have a handful of almonds and a glass of water.

Mike's Behavioral Strategy for Creativity

Mike discovered that his challenge with exercise was not a matter of disinterest or distaste with physical activity, as is the case with some people. For him it was rather a time and work-life balance issue. He struggled with balancing work priorities and his own self-care, finding himself tempted to get work done rather than making time for exercise.

He also found himself initially resistant to giving up his wine in the evening, as it still gave him a sense of comfort. The idea of losing this source of comfort was just too daunting at first.

We agreed to begin by focusing on what he felt he *could* do, and started with small steps. Instead of trying to do the lengthy triathlon sessions at the club, he would allow himself to start by attending only half-sessions, making the commitment feel more manageable. We also agreed not to worry about the wine, and instead to focus on the better food choices he was making through his revised meals and snacks.

The first few weeks were difficult for Mike, as he noticed he was a creature of habit and any change was challenging. But Mike persevered, and he managed to celebrate the small successes without letting the challenges bring him down.

As we continued our sessions together, Mike discovered a psychological element lurking beneath his struggles. He saw that he was driven by fear of aging, which made him feel as if he were losing touch with the man he used to be – the top-performing triathlete and creative machine. The older he felt, the more fearful he became. He had resorted to unhealthy behaviors as a form of defeat.

This was a great revelation, and it gave us an opportunity to connect the fear to many of his lifestyle choices. This awareness gave Mike something tangible to manage, which in turn offered a sense of power over something that had previously felt beyond his intervention.

As he learned to talk about his fears, he discovered that they were fueled by his own self-image as a "middle-aged burnout." We began to consciously shift his attention from threat to opportunity, from viewing aging as a negative to seeing the possibility of aging in a healthy, strong and athletic way.

To facilitate this shift, we began a daily gratitude ritual in which Mike would focus on celebrating all of the small wins in his day – including each time he made an effort toward being healthier.

Over time, through this practice, Mike began to notice that his self-improvement efforts and new lifestyle choices gave him much more pleasure than the occasional self-destructive lapse into an old unhealthy habit.

Results

Over the course of the first four weeks, Mike started to notice considerable improvements in his energy levels, as well as in his weight. As his waistline began to shrink, he began to feel more relaxed. He started to discover that managing his performance as he grows older is very much in his control.

As he reclaimed that power by becoming healthier, he also noticed that this empowerment crossed over into his daily work habits. His increase in energy, for example, had enabled him to put more effort into his organizational skills, making him more effective and freeing up time. His team began to respond to him differently as a result of his new attitude and outlook. Playtime at work was an instant hit with his team, and team members naturally started collaborating with each other more as a result.

He also noticed that, as a result of playtime, his team members began to involve him more in conversations about creative processes. This inclusion made Mike feel like he was part of the creative family once again.

Mike was finally having fun at work, and he looked forward to going to work each day. He felt reinvigorated. And with that shift he began to notice new creative ideas coming to him naturally and spontaneously as they had in the past.

As the months went by, Mike lost a tremendous amount of weight and began to see his old triathlete self in the mirror – affirming that he wasn't so much aging as simply maturing like a fine wine.

Speaking of wine, Mike eventually discovered, as his health and energy improved, that drinking wine wasn't as enjoyable to him anymore. He simply did not like the way he felt after drinking alcohol. He was enjoying feeling athletic again, and he discovered that after drinking wine, that feeling quickly faded.

Instead of spending his evening downtime drinking with his wife, they decided to take up yoga together. He and his wife grew even closer, which was a lovely and unexpected side effect. Mike was reminded of how much he and his wife enjoyed each other's company. They even felt that the yoga they did together rekindled old romantic feelings in them both – feelings he had assumed (again, mistakenly) would deteriorate with age.

One year later, during a follow-up meeting, Mike told me that he had entered his first mini-triathlon. He exclaimed that his creativity has returned, and he's reclaimed his famed reputation for being the creative wizard at work. His relationship with his wife is better than ever.

Thanks to creativity-boosting healthy exercise and nutrition strategies, Mike is a man transformed, who is living the life he deserves.

Chapter Twelve

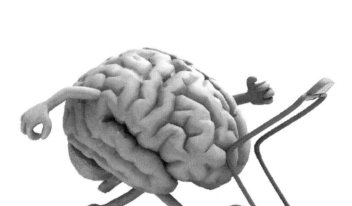

Change and Performance

"It is not the strongest or the most intelligent who will survive but those who can best manage change."

Charles Darwin

In previous chapters, I've discussed how the brain works, how stress and arousal impact our behavior, how to bring the brain into a focused state and how to improve creativity. How can we utilize all of these insights and practices to drive individual and organizational change?

Anyone who has experience with introducing any type of new initiative into an organization – or who is trying to change his or her own behavior – will probably agree that making behavior changes that stick for a long period of time, can be extremely challenging. For many of us, it can even seem practically impossible. In fact, research has shown repeatedly that both organizational *and* individual change initiatives fail in 70 percent of the cases.

Why is it that brains are so resistant to change?

Let's look at an example that may not be directly related to business, but offers an understanding of how challenging change can be for the brain: the obesity problem in the United States.

According to the Centers for Disease Control and Prevention, approximately 70 percent of the U.S. population is overweight, and more than 30 percent is obese. In a nation of more than 300 million people, that's a lot of excess weight.

Obesity is, of course, not limited to the U.S. According to the World Health Organization, Mexico just took first place as the fattest nation in the world, with the U.S. a close second. These are followed by Chile, Australia, England, Brazil, Sweden and Norway. In fact, obesity is fast becoming a global epidemic.

Fortunately for us, the United States has been following and researching the obesity epidemic in its country for more than 30 years, providing us with valuable data from which to learn.

A popular belief is that weight management is simply a matter of consuming less calories than we expend, and with a bit of self-discipline, anyone can easily lose weight.

Yet with such staggering obesity statistics – and with our knowledge about the brain, motivation and behavior – a different picture should be emerging. It has become clear that the obesity problem is not merely about calories in and calories out, or about individuals choosing to eat the wrong foods.

No matter how hard people try to eat healthy and introduce exercise into their lives, many eventually fall back into old habits. In 2000, Danish researchers concluded that 85 percent of people who try to lose weight end up regaining their weight within three years.

Interestingly, they also discovered that people who underwent behavioral therapy increased their chances of success in the long run. This suggests that the brain plays a fundamental role in a person's ability to change behavior and maintain that behavior change over longer periods of time.

The Brain and Behavior Change

In his 1949 book, "The Organization of Behavior," Donald Hebb proposed a neuroscientific mechanism that occurs during the learning process. In this phenomenon, neurons repeatedly fire together and eventually *wire together*, creating a new neurological pathway that neurons subsequently prefer. The new pathway becomes the dominant pathway.

This phenomenon is described as *Hebb's rule,* and lies at the foundation of neuroplasticity. In principle, neuroplasticity is the rewiring of the brain as an adaptive response to a stimulus.

Initially, when learning any new behavior, neurons in the brain are often forced to seek connections with other neurons in a completely different part of the brain. It can cost the brain a great deal of energy to establish the connection for the very first time. Once the connection is made, however, it will require less energy for the brain to follow that same pathway. Repeated stimulation of that newly formed pathway makes the pathway gradually stronger until it becomes so strong that it's the new preferred pathway for the brain.

One analogy I like to use is this: think about a herd of elephants about to make their way through the jungle. The first elephant must expend a lot of energy pushing over trees and navigating its way from one side of the jungle to the next. Once through, the second elephant will naturally choose the same path as the first elephant because it costs less energy to follow the path already created than to create its own path.

Every elephant in the herd will naturally follow the path of least resistance, plodding along the path created by the first elephant. What's more, after about 200 elephants have passed through, the jungle path is not just a little path anymore, but the size of a highway. In fact, the path has become so wide, that every single land-based animal in the jungle chooses that path to travel from one side of the jungle to the other.

Learning happens in much the same way. The first time we practice a new behavior, neurons must navigate their way through the jungle of 100 billion neurons in the brain to find the right ones necessary to exhibit that behavior, much like the first elephant. However, with every new repetition, that pathway becomes a little bit stronger and it costs the brain less energy to follow that pathway.

Eventually, over time and with enough repetition, that pathway becomes a highway – and much like the highway in the jungle, it becomes the highway of choice, thus solidifying that new behavior.

Unfortunately for us, however, nature has added a level of complexity. In his 2009 book, "Dynamic Energy Budget Theory for Metabolic Organisation," Dutch scientist Professor Bas Kooijman explains that every animal on this planet has a primary survival mechanism embedded in its subconscious: to conserve and store energy in order to maintain survival fitness despite changing environmental conditions.

What this means is that the brain is not fond of expending unnecessary energy, and will resist the expenditure of energy wherever it can. If the subconscious brain can't see value in expending the energy, it will resist doing so.

Like all animals, humans possess this instinct to conserve energy wherever possible. The human brain evolved by prioritizing immediate threats to avoid. This instinct, a highly effective survival mechanism when food sources were rare, has enabled us to create a living environment where we hardly need to expend energy anymore. Our primal instinct has driven us to become a sedentary species to the extent that extreme movement is no longer a requirement.

Because this need is subconsciously driven, we're often not consciously aware of the decisions we make that are based on this evolutionary instinct. A simple example is the choice many people make to take an escalator versus powering themselves up the stairs.

A few years ago, I was with my family at Universal Studios in Los Angeles. One of the main attractions is the Studio Tour. The bus tour gives visitors a behind-the-scenes look at the studio's back lot, with a few entertaining surprises along the way. The start and end of the tour is located at a lower level in the theme park, which is reached via stairs and escalators.

After exiting the tour, my family and I stood still and watched in amazement at a long line of other visitors standing and waiting patiently to take the escalator up to the theme park. Both the up and down escalators were packed with people. Separating the two escalators was a lonely set of stairs that was not being used.

Visitors preferred to stand in line to wait for the escalator rather than climb the stairs. Even though taking the stairs would have been much quicker and healthier, their brains simply did not even consider taking the stairs – because taking the stairs costs more energy than taking the escalator. Those of us who do take the stairs have probably learned, through repeated practice, to override the brain's natural impulse to conserve energy.

I'm sure some of those visitors who were waiting in line for the escalator considered taking the stairs instead of an escalator at some point in their lives. They may even have considered starting an exercise program. Like with so many of us, they probably started their lifestyle change with great enthusiasm. However, after a few days or a few weeks, their enthusiasm evaporated (for some strange reason), leaving them more demotivated and possibly demoralized, thus pushing them back into their old default behavior.

The brain's natural desire to conserve energy is immensely strong, and if the brain does not buy in to this whole "physical activity idea," then it will do everything it can to make sure we fail miserably and fall back to our energy-conserving behaviors, such as taking the escalator over the stairs and choosing the couch over the gym.

In the workplace we also see many examples in which learning new behaviors, or starting new initiatives, are at first received with great enthusiasm – but consistent application fails to materialize or eventually falls into oblivion.

I have witnessed this happen at the leadership level as well as on the ground in many organizations, and I have witnessed this time and time again with private clients who desperately seek change in their health behaviors.

If the brain cannot see how the perceived cost of expending energy will outweigh the perceived benefit of conserving energy, it will resist any attempt to change, no matter how valiant that attempt might be.

So, the million-dollar question is: How can we get the brain to "buy in" – to perceive and believe that the cost of energy is worth the investment to change? The million-dollar answer lies in human emotion.

Emotion and Behavior Change

I'm sure we can all remember instances in which we only needed to do something once to learn a lesson for the rest of our lives – versus having to practice a behavior for years that still doesn't come naturally. In most cases, if we examine the circumstances, we'll find that emotion or strong feeling is what made the difference.

A simple example of this comes from my own family life. Until my daughter Kilani was about 4 years old, we had the hardest time teaching her to brush her teeth twice a day. As a typical toddler, she just didn't get what the fuss was about. It took probably a good two years of daily reminders and teeth-brushing games before Kilani started to brush her teeth twice a day without needing to be prompted.

Of course, this took a lot of patience, and we can safely say that Kilani's brain had a hard time buying in to the value of expending energy on regular brushing.

On the other hand, when Kilani was about the same age, there was also an instance in which she learned a lifelong lesson instantly. At that time, whenever someone was cooking, Kilani was always extremely curious about our stove. Each time she would reach up and try to touch the blue flames on the burner, we would tell her that touching the blue flame would hurt.

But at that young age, Kilani had no frame of reference for the word *hurt*, so our efforts fell on deaf ears. One day, when I was cooking and walked away from the stove briefly to grab something out of the refrigerator, I heard a terrible scream. I turned my head to see Kilani crying at the stove, holding her little hand.

I quickly moved her over to the sink and ran cold water on her finger. Luckily, the burn wasn't bad and she healed fast, but she never tried to touch the stove again. To this day, as a young woman, Kilani is still very cautious with the flames on the stove.

What happened in her young brain was a perfect example of how an intense emotional event can instantly develop neural pathways that stay active for a lifetime. Kilani's perception of pain was so intense that it evoked a major fear response. This resulted in immediate long-term learning – a lesson so strong that it has lasted decades, and will probably last a lifetime.

Of course, this doesn't mean that pain and fear are good teaching tools for a child. On the contrary, purposely instilling fear in a child as a learning mechanism has long been shown to cause unnecessary trauma, and can result in post-traumatic stress disorders and many other psychological problems.

However, what Kilani learned that day from her traumatic stove experience was a simple evolutionary and acute survival mechanism – the kind that teaches us not to repeat a certain behavior if it causes bodily harm. On that day, it was a good lesson for Kilani.

What we can learn from this is that the speed at which we learn a new behavior is influenced by our emotional involvement. If we are not emotionally invested in learning – for example, brushing our teeth – it takes longer for that behavior to become a habit.

Emotion is therefore the "volume button" of learning. Our ability to access the right emotional triggers can accelerate behavior change and increase our chances of maintaining those behaviors in the long term.

Are negative emotions, such as fear, anxiety, anger and sadness, the only "volume buttons" for learning? Not at all. Research in the field of positive psychology is showing us that the effects of positive emotions on learning and behavior change are actually much more powerful.

In his 2009 article in the "Oxford Review of Education," University of Pennsylvania's Dr. Martin Seligman explains that the excitement or joy we feel about pursuing something that makes us happy – and the rewards we get from that pursuit – instill a much stronger effect on learning than the avoidance of a negative consequence.

Now let's put this in the context of long-term weight management and related behaviors. In a 2012 review article published in the "International Journal of Behavioral Nutrition and Physical Activity," author Pedro Teixeira and colleagues explain that most people trying to lose weight decide to do so as a result of external – or *extrinsic* – goals, such as improving attractiveness, conforming to social norms of thinness, responding to instruction from a doctor or minimizing discrimination from others.

According to the authors, such motives have a much lower long-term success rate than motives that are *intrinsic*, such as a desire to be healthier or for the purpose of self-growth.

Many of the extrinsic motives also tend to be results-driven, pursuant to outcomes such as a number on the scale. Intrinsic motivators tend to be more process-driven, fueled by experiences such as the enjoyment of the journey rather than a focus on the destination.

In other words, a healthy and positive outlook that evokes positive emotions and focuses on self-growth in the process will lead to a much stronger sense of motivation. And that motivation will most likely last longer than short-term goal-specific motives fueled by avoiding negative emotions.

This positive, process-driven approach is known as *self-determination*. By increasing the "volume" of emotions that are fueled by positive thinking and self-growth, we become more capable of adopting new behaviors for a longer period of time. This in turn may greatly increase the strength of the newly formed neural connections in the brain, thus increasing the possibility that the new behavior will become the new default behavior preferred by the brain.

Of course, there are times when an extrinsic motivator can trigger the emotional realization that a new behavior is necessary. This can function as a powerful kickstarter. Even so, once the new behavior is adopted, motivation levels tend to drop rapidly shortly after. Without a backup plan to transform the negative, extrinsic motivator into a positive, intrinsic one – the duration of the newly learned behavior is likely to be short-lived.

For example, I once had a client who was the CEO of a multinational finance group. He was extremely overweight. He drank heavily and ate everything in sight. It appeared that there was not a soul on earth who could convince him to change his ways, and he had made enough money to support the next three generations of his bloodline.

One thing my client loved more than anything else was his family. He absolutely adored his wife and kids. Even so, his family's concerns about his health could never get him to take better care of himself.

One day, however, a little miracle occurred. On a Sunday morning, his 7-year-old son Max walked into the kitchen and gave his dad a hug, then looked up at him and said, "You know, Dad, I really miss giving you big hugs."

"What do you mean?" his dad asked. "Well," replied Max, "I used to be able to get my arms all around you and give you a *big* hug, but now my hands don't touch behind your back."

The idea of depriving his son of the ability to give him a full hug had such a tremendous emotional impact on my client that he instantly stopped all unhealthy behaviors and started eating right and exercising.

In his brain, the first motivational trigger was a negative emotion – the sadness that he felt about what his son had said. But once he made the decision to turn his health around, positive and happy emotions fueled his resolve to change. He began to envision the joy he would give himself and his son once he reached the point when his son could give him that full, all-the-way-around hug. (Although at this point his motive was positive, it was result-driven, so it was still not quite the strongest motive.)

After a few months, my client achieved his goal and his son was able to give him that full hug again. The immense joy he saw in his son's eyes, and the amazingly positive emotion he felt as a result, helped solidify his decision to never let his health and body get so out of control again.

Interestingly, he also began to enjoy how good it felt to be healthy, which became another intrinsic motivator that focused on the process (the energy and sense of well-being that health provides) rather than on the result of a smaller waistline.

Years later, I still hear from this man once in a while and he is still taking care of himself and loving his newfound health. His brain learned to see that the benefits of healthy eating and exercise far outweigh the previously perceived "benefits" or "pleasures" that constituted an unhealthy life. His healthy behaviors have taken the place of the old unhealthy behaviors and have become the new default.

The Integrated Model of Change

More than 60 years ago, Kurt Lewin – one of the pioneers of social psychology and organizational change theories – developed a three-step process for change that sounds much simpler than it actually is.

According to Lewin, we must first "unfreeze" our resistance, so we can be receptive to the idea of change. Then, we can execute the intended change. And finally, to ensure that those changes become permanent, we need to "refreeze" the new behavior. This was the beginning of our understanding that change is not necessarily a spontaneous event, but is in fact a process. Sometimes, the speed of the change process can seem very short like an event. Other times, it can be a process spanning over many months, years or even generations.

Over the past six decades, much research has been done on the psychological drivers involved in the process of change, and one of the most commonly used models to date is the "Transtheoretical Stages of Change."

The Transtheoretical Stages of Change model, developed by James Prochaska and Carlo DiClemente in the 1970s, illustrates a progressive model of stages that an individual travels through to reach a point of readiness to change. They created this model while working in the health field – my field. Their interest was in the improvement of health behavior. But this model has held true for decades and it is universally applicable to any change.

The Transtheoretical Stages of Change model consists of five stages: pre-contemplation, contemplation, preparation, action and maintenance.

In the **pre-contemplation** stage, there's no awareness of the need to change. Using obesity as an example, somebody who is overweight in this stage will *not* be thinking about losing weight.

Contemplation is the recognition of the need to change – but without a commitment to any meaningful action. Contemplation could be triggered by an extrinsic motivator, such as feedback from a colleague or hearing from the doctor that one needs to lose weight.

In this stage, an overweight person will recognize the need to lose weight but does not yet take any meaningful steps in that direction. The brain is trying to sort out whether the benefits of behavior changes are worth the energy, and if they outweigh the payoffs of not changing behavior.

The length of time someone resides in contemplation will depend on how great the emotional response was to the extrinsic motivator. As we've seen, the greater the emotional response, the stronger the motivation and learning – and the sooner someone may consider actually taking the necessary steps.

Once people make the decision to change a behavior, they enter into the next stage: the **preparation** stage. In this stage, a commitment to change behavior is accompanied by preparation for action. An overweight person in this stage might sign up for a membership at the gym, or enroll in a nutrition course – but would not yet have attended either.

In the **action** stage, people actually act to change behavior. Here's where an overweight person would begin to engage in healthier behaviors, such as choosing healthier foods, eating less, working out or a combination of these.

Finally, in **maintenance**, changes are reinforced and sustained. This is a crucial stage in behavior change. The majority of people who make a conscious change in behavior don't sustain it if they are unable to transition from extrinsic motivation to an intrinsic one.

For example, losing weight because the doctor urged it might work for a short while, but the behaviors required to sustain it are unlikely to last if that remains the sole motivator.

Putting effort into focus on intrinsic motivators will continually reinforce the benefits of the behavior change, ensuring a much more long-lasting effect. This effort could include focusing on the enjoyment of exercise, how good we feel when we eat healthy foods, or how much better we perform at work with more energy.

Prochaska and DiClemente do caution that people don't necessarily move smoothly through these stages. They can be stuck in one stage or another for a long time, or may even skip a stage. Moreover, we can move backward through the stages – also known as a *relapse*. Relapse often occurs when the brain simply stops seeing the benefits of the behavior change.

For example, when we start realizing how much effort goes into losing just a little bit of weight, or grow tired of our exercise routine, or weary of worrying about making healthy food choices, the brain slowly starts reactivating old neurological pathways from old behavioral habits. Especially in the early stages of change, those older pathways will still require much less energy than the new pathways, resulting in a relapse to those old behaviors.

Eventually, if relapse is prolonged, we can potentially re-enter the pre-contemplation or contemplation stage.

In 2004, organizational change expert Jeff Hiatt developed the ADKAR Model – the organizational change equivalent of the Transtheoretical Stages of Change. ADKAR stands for **A**wareness, **D**esire, **K**nowledge, **A**bility and **R**einforcement.

In his book, "ADKAR: A Model for Change in Business, Government and Our Community," Hiatt explains that **awareness** is the first requirement for change. That awareness needs to be turned into **desire**, which in turn feeds into the need for **knowledge**, which leads to a sense of empowerment, resulting in a sense of **ability**. Then change is **reinforced** through continued repetition.

There are parallels between these "stages of change" models, as this illustration shows. And the stages in each model not only parallel each other, but complement and interact in interesting ways. We can consider the connections between these two models to be an *integrated model of change.*

Someone who is in the pre-contemplation stage, who is not yet thinking about a need to change, needs to become aware in order to move forward. Without awareness, there can be no desire. Desire leads to preparation – and brains that are prepared to change are more receptive to knowledge. Knowledge then empowers a sense of ability, which leads to action. When a new behavior is repeated and reinforced positively, it's likely to be maintained and thus to become the new norm.

These two models are complementary and together provide us with a powerful road map for any change-management initiative.

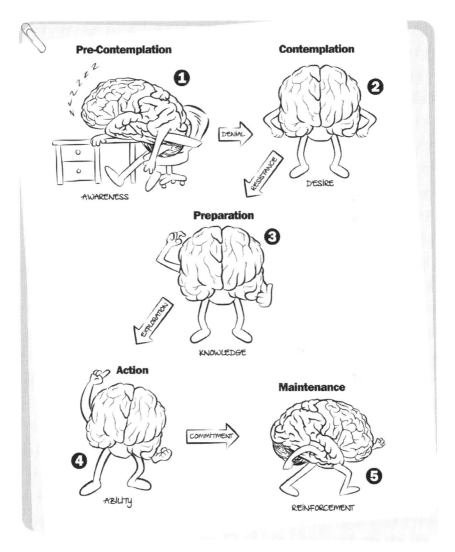

Whether we're seeking a health behavior change or an organizational policy change, employees in the pre-contemplation stage may initially be resistant because their brains simply don't see the need or the benefit – the payoff may not be perceived by the brain as worth the energy expenditure. This population of people will require a strategy that cultivates enough awareness to trigger an emotional drive to change.

Not all employees will reside in the pre-contemplation stage regarding a given initiative. Another group of employees may already be in the contemplation stage, recognizing the need but not having made a commitment. Some may be preparing (but need knowledge), and perhaps even a small group of people may be in the action stage already and are applying themselves accordingly. The latter group might still need some reinforcement to support maintenance.

This means that when implementing any change strategy, we need to be aware of where our employees reside in each phase of these integrated models of change, so we can address each group. Effective change management initiatives include appropriate strategies for each group.

Now we know how the brain tends to resist change unless it can "buy in" to the idea that change is worth the effort – and that it is possible for the brain to develop new neural pathways as it proceeds through the integrated model of change. It's worth exploring whether or not we can train our brains to rewire themselves *more quickly and with less resistance.*

The short (and exciting) answer to that is yes. And one of the best ways to train our brains to become more adaptable to change is through exercise and nutrition.

Chapter Thirteen

Strategies to Drive Change

"Change is inevitable. Growth is optional."
John C. Maxwell

In previous sections we explored how exercise and nutrition build brain cells, improve energy reserves and support neurotransmitter availability. One could say these benefits build *capacity*.

But capacity for change alone is not enough to create change in the brain. New neural pathways will only occur when relevant behavior change forces those neurons to seek new connections.

We also have seen that learning new behaviors can be extremely time-consuming. This can make learning new behaviors at work a costly affair.

In this book, I have compared executive performance to athlete performance. But athletes spend much of their time training and practicing new skills and behaviors, and only a small percent of time actually performing on the world stage. For the average executive, this ratio is reversed: generally, more time is spent performing rather than training.

Athletes aren't the only high-performing professionals who spend more of their time training than performing. The same is true for airline pilots and fighter pilots.

When fighter pilots prepare for battle, or learn to fly new jets, they're not thrown into multimillion-dollar jets first, for obvious reasons. To prepare for operational readiness, pilots spend numerous hours in flight simulators where they practice maneuvers and are confronted with various scenarios. This is how they learn the behaviors necessary to complete essential missions that help win battles and minimize casualties.

Even when maneuvers have been mastered, and after thousands of hours of actual flight time under their belts, pilots still need to spend a minimum number of hours in a flight simulator each year to ensure they sustain mastery.

In fact, a recent story by the Canadian Television Network (CTV) mentioned that fighter pilots spend more than 20 percent of their flying time in a simulator, and military leadership is looking into increasing simulation time to at least 50 percent of flight time in hopes of decreasing operational costs while maintaining skill.

How is this relevant for the average executive? Well, think about this. What if there was a "simulator" where an executive could spend time learning maneuvers and behaviors that would help win "battles" over the competition, minimize damage in the workplace and decrease operational costs? Surely, such a "simulator" would offer an extremely high return on investment.

Here's the great news: there is, in effect, such a simulator. It's exercise and the practice of healthy nutrition. Neuroscience is teaching us that this is the way in which exercise and nutrition may offer the greatest benefit of performance.

There are, of course, many other benefits, too. We've seen that exercise and nutrition make employees healthier, more resilient against stress, better focused and more creative, which in turn makes them better performers.

But the rigors, habits and practices inherent in exercise and nutrition can also function as powerful simulators in which people "rehearse" behaviors that are essential for success in business.

Many of the same neural circuits involved in changing exercise and nutrition behaviors are also necessary for changing our behaviors in the workplace and in daily life. During exercise, and when managing our nutrition, we learn many critical skills and flex many capacities and abilities that serve our learning in the workplace – managing discomfort, staying cool under pressure, acknowledging and communicating feelings without behaving emotionally, and building adaptability.

For example, while challenging ourselves to learn a new exercise, we may need to learn how to manage our frustrations. Or as we adapt to a healthier diet, we might practice managing our impulses to give in to the temptation of junk food.

The internal dialogue that ensues in these instances is often the same dialogue that occurs when dealing with the frustration of learning a new work skill, or managing the temptation of a distractor while in the middle of a project.

By matching similar behavioral characteristics and repeating them over and over again during exercise, or while we're practicing healthy eating, we're able to make the brain more adaptable to changing those neural pathways. As the brain becomes more adaptable, the brain will require less energy expenditure to develop those new neural pathways – and thus be less resistant to change.

This makes exercise and nutrition supremely valuable change management tools in any organization.

Your Road Map for Change

As discussed in the previous chapter, change can be a challenging process requiring full commitment and emotional buy-in from the brain. But even after the brain buys in to the idea of change, we aren't home free. Once we embark on a journey of change, we often find ourselves challenged by the elements of life – almost as if they are deliberately trying to sabotage our best intentions to change.

I've observed just how typical this is through my work with clients, many of whom reached the "action phase" described previously and jumped in with both feet, expecting smooth sailing – only to find themselves landing on the hard ground of reality before they were able to set sail.

The truth is, life is full of uncontrollable situations. We need to learn to navigate these and stay on course in our "new sailing boat" so we can achieve our goals. Desire, knowledge and ability are foundational for learning new behaviors – especially for getting started. But there are additional capacities that will see us through the process.

To help my clients navigate through the challenges of life while trying to learn a new behavior, I developed a behavioral road map that I like to call: the **PRIMAL Model of Success**.

The "PRIMAL" in the PRIMAL Model of Success is both an acronym as well as a reminder that within our brains resides that primitive portion, the limbic system, which needs to "buy in" to the change, if behavior change is desired. Furthermore, the limbic brain is largely responsible for our emotions, and as discussed in the previous chapter, emotional involvement is the "volume button" for learning new behaviors. Interestingly, the word PRIMAL also serves as a perfect acronym to describe the six traits, or skills, that are shared by most successful people and organizations.

PRIMAL stands for: **P**urposeful, **R**esourceful, **I**ndustrious, **M**asterful, **A**ccepting and **L**iberated. I developed this model during my years of researching leadership. In my own research,

I consistently observed that the most successful people and organizations exhibited certain skills and traits that allowed them to succeed where others didn't.

As I looked closely at their behaviors, I began to see that certain Olympic athletes, movie stars, human rights activists and successful business people all tend to instinctively apply these same six skills or capacities to achieve success.

Many of these individuals apply these six skills across many different aspects of their lives, not just their primary sport or vocation. That's why an athlete like famed NBA star Magic Johnson is equally successful in business as he was in sports, because he applies the same skills in his business pursuits as he applied to be a successful athlete.

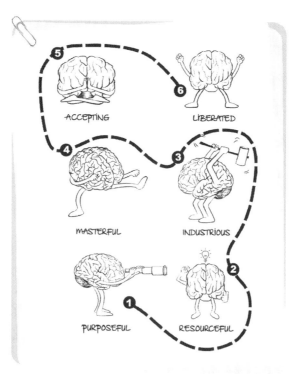

By learning from their examples, we can apply these skills and cultivate these capacities to achieve success in whatever *we* are pursuing – whether it's weight loss, health improvement, business performance or exceptional living.

Purposeful: Being purposeful means that every decision and every behavior is geared toward achieving objectives. It's about our ability to keep the eye on the ball, and to make sure that the decisions we make on a daily basis are in line with our change objectives. It's about remaining attentive and ensuring that our actions are relevant to our goals.

The essence of purposefulness is always being aware of how any action or decision is related to the overall objective. If a current action is not related to the objective, its value needs to be seriously scrutinized.

Using a wellness objective as an example, let's assume someone wants to lose 20 pounds. Every single day – whether traveling, in the office or at home, sick or healthy – every single decision made about eating and movement must be made with that purpose in mind. That goal is the lens through which all health- and fitness-related decisions are considered.

Any time a situation presents itself that could possibly steer that person off course, the question must be asked: "Is the decision I'm making right now going to help me lose 20 pounds?"

Teams as well as individuals can be purposeful. When I have conversations with my teams, sometimes I ask, "Is this conversation helping to get us where we want to be?" If it's not, we change the conversation to one with relevance to the goal.

The ability to be purposeful is essential because it keeps us on course to achieve our performance goals.

Resourceful: In his book, "The Leader's Pocket Guide – 101 Indispensible Tools, Tips, and Techniques for Any Situation," author John Baldoni explains that resourcefulness involves the ability to know what resources are necessary for change, and to ensure that they are available. This can be achieved either by creating new resources where there are none, or by making old resources work better. This could include physical tools as well as time, energy, emotion and perspective.

Let's take the wellness objective from the previous section as an example. One essential resource that we need in order to take better care of ourselves and to exercise regularly is time. Yet, time is something that we always seem to have too little of. In my coaching and workshops, the number one argument why participants do not exercise is the perception of limited time. Truthfully, we are all given the same 24 hours per day, so it's not about having enough time, but rather what are we spending our 24 hours per day on? If we are spending those 24 hours on everything else other than exercise, then we will never have enough time.

Resourcefulness requires taking a closer look at that resource of time and critically analyzing our time management to see if it's possible to restructure our timetables so we can create a window of opportunity to exercise. Our ability to do this successfully often requires a healthy dose of creativity, which was discussed in some depth in Chapters 9-11.

Industrious: Merriam-Webster defines *industrious* as "constantly, regularly, or habitually active or occupied; diligent." Another way of saying "industrious" might be "hardworking" – in a steady, devoted, energetic and conscientious manner.

There's no question about it: working hard is a prerequisite for success. There's a certain amount of blood, sweat and tears involved in every success story.

But industriousness is not only about working hard – it's about working *smart*. In other words, it has to do with energy management.

What are we spending our energy on? Think of energy as a bucket of water. If we waste 90 percent of the water on activities that aren't important, we don't have enough left for the things that really need the water.

Again, let's put this into the wellness objective example. If we allow our brains to reside constantly on the left or right side of the arousal curve, our brains spend much of their energy either seeking novelty or seeking threat, depending on whether we are on the left or right side. These distractions will cause us to expend a tremendous amount of energy to function. By the end of the day, it won't be a surprise that the brain will be exhausted. An exhausted brain does not have the capacity to manage the limbic brain's impulsive nature, making it virtually impossible to override the temptation of eating unhealthy food, drinking alcohol, and spending the evening on the couch, instead of eating healthy and exercising.

Being industrious, therefore, depends heavily on our ability to maximize our time in the performance zone of the arousal curve, by being selective about what we pay attention to, so we can conserve energy for the things that are most important.

Masterful: Mastery and expertise are not just about being good at what we do. Of course, our skill and experience are vital to mastery, but achieving true mastery is about much more. In his book, "Drive – The Surprising Truth About What Motivates Us," Dan Pink explains that mastery enables us to perform in a natural state of flow that makes our skill seem effortless and easy. With mastery, we achieve a state of relaxation and poise once we realize that our abilities outmatch our challenges.

According to Pink, mastery abides by three rules. First, it requires a growth mindset that enables us to see our abilities not as finite, but infinitely improvable. Second, pursuit of mastery requires the acceptance of discomfort, as achieving greater levels of mastery requires constant practice, grit and effort. Finally, mastery can only be pursued but never achieved. The tireless pursuit of mastery enables continued growth, which eventually allows us to outgrow our perceived challenges and limitations.

From a wellness perspective, learning a new exercise and nutritional regimen will take time to master. Initially, practicing these new behaviors will likely be challenging, and at times, even frustrating, which will require constant practice. By being purposeful, resourceful and industrious, over time we learn to master these behaviors and they become the new "normal" for us. Once at that level, we become comfortable in our new routine and begin to realize that no matter what challenges arise in life, we have mastered the skills and possess the resilience to deal with whatever comes our way. In fact, we become exceedingly more resilient as we continue to pursue mastery in our exercise and nutrition.

This resilience crosses over into other aspects of our lives, such as work, which in turn makes us appear relaxed, poised and confident, even in times of adversity.

I like to use the example of a kung fu master. Everyone knows he's an expert at what he does, but as a master, he has become so relaxed in his disposition and skills that he actually has time and energy to elevate the performance of others around him, while continuing to grow. As a master, he is an inspiration to his students and peers. He is, in fact, a leader.

The fact that wellness behaviors such as exercise translate into more effective leadership has been established in a landmark study by the Center for Creative Leadership (CCL). They conducted research on a whopping 4,000 executives who underwent CCL's trademarked 360-feedback assessment. According to CCL, a 360-feedback assessment is a method of systematically collecting opinions about an individual's performance from a wide range of co-workers. This could include peers, direct reports, the boss and the boss's peers – along with people outside the organization, such as customers. CCL's objective for collecting data of this kind is to present the executive with a panorama of perceptions about their performance, rather than just self-perception, which sets the stage for greater self-awareness and improvement.

In their research, they examined whether or not executives who exercise are possibly perceived differently than non-exercising executives. What they discovered is that executives who exercise are perceived to be better leaders, as being calmer under pressure, and appear to be more productive. This shows that by pursuing mastery in our exercise and nutrition, we inadvertently achieve greater resilience and mastery in our work as professionals and as leaders.

Accepting: Being accepting in a performance and change context is our willingness to embrace the challenges that will inevitably arise. It's about embracing the fact that things don't always go according to plan. Yes, we need to have a plan, and we need to remain purposeful – but acceptance requires the mental flexibility to acknowledge that things are not always going to go according to the plan. That helps us prepare to circumvent obstacles as they arise.

To achieve a healthy and helpful level of acceptance, we must be prepared to adapt and adjust, which requires a great deal of self-awareness, self-regulation and motivation. Daniel Goleman, author of "Emotional Intelligence," is considered by many as one of the foremost authorities in the field of organizational performance, due to his dedication to research. In a "Harvard Business Review" article, Goleman wrote that his research showed a distinct correlation between superior performance and emotional intelligence. According to Goleman, Emotional Intelligence (EQ) involves a number of competencies that are deeply rooted in our ability to know ourselves, as well as our capacity to effectively work with others. These competencies are Self-Awareness, Self-Regulation, Motivation, Empathy and Social Skills.

The first three competencies involve managing ourselves and are essential for personal performance excellence.

Self-Awareness involves our ability to reflect on our own moods, actions and emotions. With a high level of self-awareness, we are able to recognize our own responsibilities and flaws, when something does not go according to plan.

Self-Regulation is our ability to control, or redirect, inappropriate impulses that may arise from our emotions. In other words, when we recognize that something is not going according to plan, we may identify that we are beginning to feel frustrated (self-awareness). However, with a healthy dose of self-regulation, we are able to inhibit our impulse to behave in a frustrated manner and regulate those destructive impulses before we do something stupid that we might end up regretting later on.

Motivation is our drive to pursue goals that have a greater meaning than money or status. Motivation is deeply rooted in our sense of purposefulness. Remember, when the PRIMAL, or limbic, brain can emotionally buy into the goal, it will be more motivated to participate in the pursuit of that goal. The more motivated we are to succeed, the more willing we will be to regulate our frustrations and find ways to navigate around our challenges.

The final two competencies involve managing our relationships with others. These competencies are essential in team or organizational performance.

Empathy is our ability to understand the emotional makeup of others. Someone with a high level of empathy is able to imagine another person's emotions with such intensity, that they actually feel those emotions.

Finally, the competency of Social Skills involves our ability to build rapport, manage relationships and build networks. Goleman stated that much more than being friendly, being socially skillful requires friendliness with purpose that inspires people to move in the same direction we are moving.

In the context of emotional intelligence, being accepting would involve our ability to accept the emotions, challenges and frustrations of our peers, while simultaneously regulating how we respond to them. Then to effectively help our peers manage

247

their emotions so the whole team can work together to fix the problem and move on to achieve its goals.

Putting this again into a wellness context: We may have the best plans to exercise today, but out of the blue, something happens that throws our plans out the window. I have encountered many clients who became frustrated when their plans to exercise were disrupted by life's events and they ended up responding in a destructive manner by binging on junk food because they were so upset.

In aftermath, I would often get the explanation that since their exercise plans were disrupted, they lost all motivation to eat healthy as well. In a case like this, self-awareness would help us identify that we feel frustrated because we can't exercise. Self-regulation would then help us inhibit the impulse to destructively eat junk food as an act of frustration.

Finally, our sense of motivation would help to remind ourselves how important it is to achieve our goals and to think of exercise alternatives that we CAN do, rather than focusing on what we CAN'T do. In that state of motivation, we could choose to do some stairs at work, or choose to work out later on at home, instead of at the gym. These types of self-management behaviors will likely lead to a much greater level of success than by giving up each time the going gets tough.

Liberated. Liberty is the ability to make and implement one's own decisions. Research shows that having the autonomy to do things our way is, for many people, far more engaging than being told what to do. In a 2004 article published by the "Journal of Applied Social Psychology," the authors state that employees who were encouraged and supported to make their own decisions far outperformed employees who were not given such liberties.

As we discussed in Chapter 3, having the liberty to decide our own fate increases our sense of control, even in situations that seem uncontrollable. In my own practice with clients, I have experienced many situations when clients were more likely to stick to their plans if they were able to take ownership over their own strategies to become healthier. For example, when clients were given choices of a type of exercise regimen or nutrition strategy, they appeared much more compliant to their own decisions than when the exercise or nutrition was prescribed.

In my opinion, one of the greatest flaws in health care, dietetics or in personal fitness training is to prescribe health behaviors, rather than give options and choices and then to coach the client based on those choices. I remember conducting a workshop about emotion and movement at one of the largest gym chains in the United States. While explaining the research behind the power of autonomy and how making our own decisions, even about our exercise, may produce greater results, I experienced a great deal of resistance from trainers.

These trainers, who were conditioned to believe that prescribing sets and reps to clients is the only way to achieve fitness success, felt that if clients weren't "told" what to do and how hard they should work, they likely would not work hard enough. This belief was so deeply ingrained into their brains, that trainers refused to even consider the possibility that if we give clients a greater level of autonomy they may possibly work harder than when not given the autonomy.

For many professionals, the idea of giving a client more autonomy is simply frightening, which shows me that we still have a long way to go. Luckily, there were trainers who bought into the idea of autonomy, and those trainers started experimenting with giving clients choices. To their amazement, not only did the clients work harder during sessions, but the trainers discovered that they retained their clients much longer than trainers who believed in exercise prescription.

Furthermore, a number of clients who trained with the prescriptive trainers ended up transferring over to the trainers who gave more autonomy. The clients seemed to perceive the autonomous trainers as more service-oriented and as more caring than the prescriptive trainers. As months went by, a number of the prescriptive trainers began to notice the success of the autonomous trainers and one-by-one they began to conform. Finally, after about one year, the personal training culture had experienced a paradigm shift resulting in greater client retention and revenue for the company.

This is exactly what research in organizational psychology is showing us as well. Autonomy leads to greater levels of happiness, performance and revenue. And in the case of this gym chain, it was a catalyst for positive organizational change.

So, now that we have explained the theory of the PRIMAL Model of Success, let's discover what this could look like in our exercise and nutrition strategies.

PRIMAL Model of Success During Exercise

No matter what form of exercise we choose (because we are Liberated), we are likely able to push our performance to greater levels by following the PRIMAL Model of Success. For this segment, I am going to use running as an example, but this can be applied to any form of exercise.

Purposeful: Prior to the run, set goals that stretch beyond simply showing up. For example, say to yourself: "Today I am going to complete that elusive 5-kilometer run without stopping." With that goal in mind, you know that every thought and decision you make on that run need to be focused on finishing the exercise. Remembering that the PRIMAL, or limbic, brain needs to emotionally buy into that goal, so think of the reasons why achieving this 5-kilometer run is so important to you. It could be to inspire your kids or colleagues, for health reasons, or it could be to prove to yourself once and for all that you are not out of shape. Whatever the reason is, it needs to be burnt into your psyche and you want to hold on to that visualization all throughout your run. Even when the run feels tough and you may be presented with opportunities to stop, you need to maintain a clear focus on why you are doing this run.

Resourceful: Plan your route and prepare for surprises that could prevent you from achieving your goal. Think about traffic, weather, bumping into co-workers who want you to stop and chat, your phone ringing, and so on. Devise a strategy for what you plan to do to overcome each of the challenges before you go for that run. This will decrease the number of possible distractors that could inhibit you from achieving your goal. Furthermore, think about what other resources you could create to help you achieve your goal. This could be in the form of a running buddy to keep you at pace, or it could be the use of a heart-rate monitor so you can maintain a steady pace. Another type of resource could be a running app such as MapMyRun, that helps you track your running performance and routes. Any type of resource that will help you stay motivated and finish that run is fair game.

Industrious: In order to be steady, consistent and diligent in your efforts, energy management is the name of the game. You know, for example, that if you start off a run by sprinting, you will likely burn out before the finish line. Determine your intensity level and manage your energy levels while running. Paying close attention to your energy will allow you to slow down when necessary or speed up when you feel you have energy to spare. While on the run, you may encounter traffic scenarios with cars, cyclists or even other runners. Knowing that interacting with inattentive drivers or other runners who get in your way might only drain unnecessary energy, focus inward and manage your own energy so you can achieve your goal.

Masterful: Like a true master, work on improving your technique. If you're running, focus on feeling light on your feet. Take some time to educate yourself on proper running technique and running posture so you can finish that run feeling like a champion. Keep your head high and remain calm. Even if the run is becoming tiring, remain poised, keep your breathing even, and attend to placing one foot in front of the other. In the beginning, when learning how to run with proper technique, it can seem more tiring than running the way you used to run. Block out the temptation to go back to the way things were and instead remain diligent in learning how to run properly.

Over time, you will improve far beyond what you could possibly achieve without learning how to run with proper technique. When that time comes, you will not only feel like a champion, but those around you will start seeing you as a champion, which in turn might inspire them to become better versions of themselves as well.

Accepting: As you exercise, you may begin to feel tired – you may feel winded and out of breath, your energy might lag, or your muscles might feel weak. At some point, no matter how hard you try, the fatigue can make it hard to focus. You may begin to feel your brain shifting to the right of the arousal curve, leading you to focus more on the problem than the outcome. When this happens, accept the fact that you are fatigued – but instead of giving any attention to the self-destructive dialogues that may enter your mind, keep your attention on your breathing and try to shift the brain back to the center of the arousal curve.

Remember that successful performance in this run will depend on your self-awareness, ability to regulate emotions, and ability to maintain your levels of motivation. Think about your emotions and how you feel right now and then focus on inhibiting the impulse to quit. Instead, focus on why you are doing this run and try to re-engage with your purpose.

Liberated: If you reach a breaking point and really don't think you can do any more or go any further, remember that you do have the freedom to decide your fate. There is no right or wrong, just your decision. Celebrate the fact that you have the freedom to decide for yourself and then decide to finish strong.

Once you cross the finish line, and you have applied PRIMAL along the way, you have helped to train your brain. You are flexing those neurons and training them to apply PRIMAL skills and capacities in every other aspect of your life.

The PRIMAL Model of Success and Nutrition

Just as with exercise, a nutrition program that develops the qualities of PRIMAL isn't necessarily about the food itself, but rather about the practice of applying these six core skills when dealing with our nutrition.

Purposeful: Sticking with a sound nutrition program can sometimes be extremely challenging, even for the most motivated people. Most of my clients struggle daily with their nutrition, and often find themselves in a losing battle. Being purposeful about nutrition gives meaning and structure to your choices. Having a long-term objective can ground your purpose in clear parameters by tying each choice directly to your goals.

Suppose your objective is losing 20 pounds in 20 weeks. From there, you develop a nutrition plan that will get you to that point. Many of the foods discussed in previous chapters would ideally be the primary foods in your diet, for all the reasons described in those chapters.

Once your plan is established, being purposeful means that every food choice is critical to the plan. You have a framework for evaluating every choice. From the first day, you may find yourself surrounded by temptation and obstacles to good nutrition: business dinners, luncheons, long flights, office pastries, and so on. Regardless of the situation, every food you choose to eat should fit in the plan to achieve your goals. With any temptation, whether it's dessert or alcohol, ask yourself the fundamental question: Will eating this food help me achieve my goal?

Resourceful: The corporate world can be a challenging place for anyone trying to stick with a healthy nutrition program.

Business lunches, long meetings, business- class meals on the plane with a free flow of wine – this lifestyle can play havoc with anyone's attempts to be healthy.

Being resourceful in this case means being prepared for anything. For example, if you have a weakness around those cookies your assistant brings in every day, try bringing healthier snack alternatives to work, such as **Greek yogurt, fruit** or an **all-natural energy bar**. If you tend to lose the battle on the airplane, either by going hungry for long flights or indulging in free alcohol, fatty meals or even pretzels and peanuts, bring plenty of your own healthier snacks.

On a very long flight, try consuming only half of what is offered and replace the wine with lots of water. (If you struggle with jet lag, then alcohol is your worst enemy – but staying well-hydrated with water will improve brain function considerably, even if you're feeling sleepy.)

Industrious: Do we need to work at eating healthy? You bet. Be prepared to spend some time and energy on tracking your food intake. One option is to download a smartphone app that helps you track the food you're consuming, and use the app to record your food intake. Or, you can keep an old-fashioned journal.

Research has shown that many people actually consume more food (or more sugar or fat) than they think they do. Using a food-tracking app will enable you to keep much closer tabs on how much food you're consuming in a day, the quantity of nutrients, and where you may be overdoing OR underdoing it. Work smart and utilize the resources available to you.

Masterful: In the world of nutrition, knowledge is power. The more time you spend reading about and studying healthy nutrition, the more equipped you will be to handle any challenges in the future. You can learn a lot about foods that are good for your brain as well as good for your body in various ways. That's going to help you make healthier decisions.

Also, allow yourself to be inspired by those around you who manage their food intake well. Learn from the masters. One day, you too will reach a level of competence and confidence in which no situation will be too challenging for you to make healthy choices.

Accepting: No matter how hard you try, there will be times when life throws a curve ball – and even the best-laid plans go out the window. At those times, it can be tempting to decide that all is lost and you might as well quit. But instead of thinking of the curve ball as a sign to quit, treat it as a brain-building exercise that's helping the neurons in your brain become better and stronger. Treat the challenge as a positive one by accepting that, although things aren't perfect right now, that doesn't mean you have to lie down in defeat.

Look for the lesson in the challenge: what can you learn from it for next time? By focusing on silver linings and the things we *can* do, we rewire the brain to do this in the future. We also regain a sense of control.

Liberated: Finally, wake up every single day with the knowledge that you have a *choice* about how you are going to live your life that day. Many people wake up, get up, go to work, come home and go to bed again at the end of the day without contemplating or acknowledging that they have choices about how they live. In my opinion, when we don't take the liberty to make a *conscious* decision about how we are going to live, that's not living – it's merely *existing*.

Instead, the moment you wake up, make a clear and decisive commitment to live life today to its fullest – and that starts with the foods you're putting into your body. Visualize the choices you'll be making throughout the day, and keep reminding yourself that these are *your* choices.

During business meals or on a flight, exercise your liberty to make healthier food choices, even when you are presented with all types of tempting foods. I once had a client who was a senior executive at a global IT firm who was struggling with his weight. In his position, he had to entertain many of his company's clients, which involved eating and drinking copious amounts of food and alcohol every day. His argument was that in his field, it would not be acceptable to feed his clients salad and sparkling water.

During one of our meetings, we spoke about the liberty to choose and he came to the realization that he could order the food and alcohol for his clients, but he didn't have to eat and drink it all. Instead, I asked him to start focusing on what he could do in a situation like that and he decided for himself that he could easily cut down the quantity of food and alcohol, but wouldn't be able to cut it out completely. By owning his decision to cut down his portions, we agreed on a strategy that before he would begin eating, he would take three deep breaths and while breathing, say to himself the following affirmation: "I choose to nourish my body and fuel my brain because I'm worth it."

Interestingly, this affirmation acted as a little reminder to make healthier choices and to limit his portions. Because it was his decision, it was easier for him to comply with his affirmation. Without much effort, he began to consume smaller amounts, which resulted in weight loss over time, and this was very empowering for him. After two months, during one of our follow-up coaching calls, he was excited about his weight loss and exclaimed that he was beginning to enjoy the newfound power over his fate. As his weight came down, his confidence went up and he began to focus on other things he could do, such as including regular exercise into his day.

Eventually, on his own terms, he transformed into the envy of his office as his self-confidence and increased energy also translated into an improvement in productivity and performance at work. Finally, many of his clients, whom he perceived required excessive wining and dining, expressed how inspiring he was and began to show interest in his health choices, resulting in them choosing to make healthier choices during their dinners as well. One could say, my client's self-directed transformation not only improved his performance, but inspired those around him to also make healthier choices.

In closing, the PRIMAL Model of Success can be your road map to greater success and superior performance. Not only is it your road map, also remember that it is your flight simulator that trains the neural circuits in your brain that are necessary for performance success. As those neural circuits become stronger through exercise and nutrition, your brain will require less effort to adapt to other changes in your life, such as changes at work, at home or in sports. With the right training, your brain will become primed to performance success, enabling you to achieve anything you set your mind to achieve.

Chapter Fourteen

Susan: A Case Study in Change

"The price of doing the same old thing is far higher than the price of change."
Bill Clinton

Susan was the CEO of a health products company based in Atlanta, Georgia. When I met her, the company had been in operation for 10 years. She was married and had a teenage daughter.

Susan's job was intense and demanding. The $30-billion-per-year health products industry was a fast-paced and competitive one. While her company offered excellent-quality products, getting the products on the shelf in health food stores was extremely challenging. There was enormous competition from a massive array of products that varied drastically in price and value, and it was often difficult for store owners and consumers to compare products.

Susan spent much of her time developing relationships with national distributors and suppliers, which necessitated a great deal of travel within the U.S.

Over the 5 years that she had been CEO, Susan won some terrific victories for the company, which resulted in steady growth. However, when we met, her company was suffering some growing pains. Expansion was necessary, but it came with costs and challenges.

For example, one of her recent wins was a distribution contract with Wal-Mart. What had not been immediately apparent was that this increase in product distribution would not automatically translate into an immediate increase in cash flow. In fact, initially it decreased cash flow.

The company's packaging, storage and transportation process was working at maximum capacity, but Wal-Mart's payment process was extremely slow. This resulted in negative cash flow and placed much stress on the company. Employees were exhausted, and her company could barely meet payroll.

Before meeting me, Susan's demanding travel schedule, long work hours and high-stress role in the company made it difficult for her to even think about exercising and eating right. She'd had a history of weight fluctuation for most of her adult life, and more recently her sleep quality had deteriorated, as her mind was constantly racing about how to re-establish a positive cash flow balance for her company.

She knew that if she kept going on her current course, her health issues would mount and her performance would suffer. Her job would have been a challenge even in perfect health. But with compromised health, she knew she could not succeed. Her role demanded high levels of energy to perform her duties.

Further, she realized that she needed to represent and model what it looked like to be the successful leader of an emerging health products company. The CEO of a company branding itself around the concept of vitality could not appear out of shape, haggard and tired – without consequences to brand image and reputation.

With this awareness, Susan had begun to research wellness and weight loss, and she felt she had come to know the subject fairly well. She knew that her nutrition had to improve, that she had to exercise regularly, and that she needed periods of rest and relaxation.

As she considered these issues, it occurred to her that she was not the only one in her company dealing with them. In fact, the more she thought about it, the more she realized that many of her employees at headquarters were in the same boat. Susan began to think that if her employees could be healthier, they too could be more resilient given the demands of the job and the uncertainty they must be feeling due to the company's financial crunch.

What if the company offered support for *everyone* to take better care of themselves – in the same ways that Susan herself knew she needed to do?

During a weekly team meeting, Susan ran the idea of some sort of wellness initiative by Bill, the Chief Finance Officer, and Karen, the Human Resources Director. Both had been with the company since its inception.

Bill's response was lukewarm. He was a "numbers guy" and not very connected with the workforce. He responded that he did not see how spending money on wellness could yield a sizable enough return on investment. To him, the wellness idea seemed like a large investment of money, time and effort that guaranteed only minimal returns.

Bill felt that there were more pressing matters requiring everyone's attention and energy before they could have the luxury of thinking about "leisure activities." He emphasized that besides the negative cash flow from the Wal-Mart contract, other sales targets were not being met, and there were still serious budget constraints preventing the company's distribution network from delivering in a timely manner. As a result, customer satisfaction was down. In his mind, these matters were most urgent and needed to be addressed before anything else.

Karen wasn't terribly enthusiastic either. She felt that a lot of the work would fall to her and her department, which was already stretched thin due to high employee turnover. Finding talent was hard enough; keeping good people for longer than a year seemed almost impossible. On top of that, the company was nearing its final quarter, which meant another round of performance appraisals, productivity reports and cultural surveys.

On a personal note, Karen herself had struggled with weight issues, especially since menopause. After a lifetime of diets, and coming from a long line of obese family members, she was resigned to being 40 pounds overweight just as she had been for her entire adult life.

Karen felt that implementing a wellness initiative at this moment would simply exhaust resources, and using her own experience as a reference, she thought that exercise programs would probably not help employees much anyway. Karen's advice was to wait for a year or two, when the company was a little more mature. Perhaps then this topic could be re-explored.

Based on the pushback from her two most trusted experts, Susan decided to shelve the idea until the time was right.

Soon after this discussion, Susan embarked on a road trip – a media tour to promote the launch of her company's new product line that would hopefully boost cash flow and close the gap on the negative cash flow from the Wal-Mart contract. While she was resting in her hotel room in Dallas one night, she began browsing the Internet and researching information about wellness and productivity.

As luck would have it, she read my online article on organizational health and behavior change. Learning that wellness not only makes employees healthier but also more productive, happier and engaged, she decided to contact me to find out more.

During our first meeting, she told me about the resistance of her CFO and HR Director to the idea of implementing a wellness campaign. She was struggling with how to convince these two people to even consider exploring a wellness initiative.

After I explained the Integrated Model of Change and how individuals move through the various stages, Susan had her first "aha" moment. She realized that she herself was in the contemplation stage, resulting in a desire to know more. Bill and Karen were in the pre-contemplation stage, thus requiring a greater level of awareness before even thinking about wellness.

As she went to bed that night, she wondered what it would take to move herself from contemplation to preparation to action – and what it would take to raise her esteemed colleagues' awareness, so they could move from pre-contemplation to contemplation or even action.

The answer wasn't long in coming. It was almost as if the universe sensed the opportunity and immediately responded. Susan was up bright and early the next day, and made her way to the local TV station for her interview on the morning show. The interview went well. She hit all her major points and felt content with her performance as she moved on to her next meeting at a local businesswomen's lunch.

When she eventually got back to the hotel, she checked the TV station's website. They had posted a video of her morning interview, and she eagerly watched it to review her performance.

Life would never be the same again.

What she saw appalled and horrified her. Whether it was the camera angle or the lighting or simply the way she was sitting, the woman she saw on TV bore no resemblance to how she saw herself. The woman she was watching looked extremely overweight, out of shape and utterly exhausted. Although she thought she had been vivacious and energetic, her visual image appeared almost lethargic. She looked tired under a thin veneer of enthusiasm.

Susan went to the bathroom, looked at herself in the mirror and cried. The emotional experience of seeing how she appeared to the world was a serious reality check. As painful as it was, it was the catalyst she needed to shift from contemplation into her planning and action stages.

She called me the next morning and told me about her experience. Susan had experienced an *extrinsic motivator*, her TV image, which had pushed her into the planning stage.

Together we discussed a strategy that would not only help her, but would also help shift her colleagues through the Integrated Transtheoretical Model of Change.

Susan's Exercise Strategy

After that extrinsic wake-up call, Susan was a woman transformed and on a mission. Even though she was traveling for business, she did not want to waste any more time. We agreed that Susan would focus on using PRIMAL as her road map. She decided to *purposely* start choosing hotels that had decent gyms with a usable collection of cardiovascular equipment, such as treadmills and stationary bikes, as well as strength training equipment such as weight machines and free weights. Each day that she wasn't flying, she would complete at least 30 minutes of cardio and an additional 20 minutes of strength training.

Whenever she felt tired or her brain would tell her that she was too busy, she would remind herself to remain *purposeful* in her objective to become healthier. This strategy helped her exercise even on days when her schedule was looking impossible.

Because her travel schedule was so intense, she spent a lot of time at the airport. Utilizing her *resourcefulness*, Susan came up with a strategy that would help her exercise even at the airport. On days that she had to fly, she would spend 30 minutes of her preboarding time walking through the airport to increase her exercise.

Over the next few weeks, Susan remained *industrious* in her efforts and gave her workouts all she had. She began to feel more confident in her workouts as they began to feel easier, which increased her sense of *mastery*.

She even began to notice that other travelers in the hotel and airport were beginning to approach her and ask questions about her exercise, which she would gladly answer. She found this sharing of knowledge invigorating, which in turn increased her motivation.

Slowly but surely, her motivation shifted from being extrinsic (focusing on her exterior) to intrinsic as she began to enjoy how it felt to exercise and to be a positive influence on her peers.

Even though she had the best intentions to exercise daily, of course there were times when life and work simply got in the way. Susan recalled that when this had happened in the past, she would simply give up and resort to treating herself with junk food and alcohol.

After learning about the power of *accepting*, however, Susan simply accepted when things didn't work out on a particular day and remained purposeful overall, returning to her core routines without becoming distracted by negativity.

As a CEO, Susan didn't take instructions very well. She much preferred to own her decisions rather than being told what to do. So we agreed that Susan would be allowed a sense of feeling *liberated* by creating her own objectives before each exercise session. If she felt more like doing cardio than strength, that was her decision to make. This worked well, since as long as she was doing *some* form of exercise, she was reaping benefits.

She likewise had the freedom to decide what type of cardio she would do. Whether she wanted to spend her time on the treadmill or stationary bike, skipping rope, or taking a dance class, the choice was entirely up to her. She enjoyed this sense of freedom, which increased her motivation further and decreased the likelihood of boredom.

Susan's Nutrition Strategy

Our first objective was for Susan to be more purposeful with her food choices. For the rest of her national tour, she agreed to stop drinking sodas and replace them with water. Every time she craved a sweet drink, she followed my advice to ask herself the question: "How is this soda going to help me regain control over my life?" This strategy worked for her and she began to feel encouraged.

Being able to make healthy food choices consistently can be extremely challenging while traveling. By focusing on being more resourceful and industrious, Susan prepared healthy snacks ahead of time. She purchased nuts, raisins and organic energy bars to ensure that she had regular access to healthy food options, rather than relying on airport and airplane food that often made her feel bloated and lethargic.

Over time, Susan felt like she was getting a grip on her food choices, and this level of mastery bolstered her confidence to continue. Whenever she encountered a challenge with her nutrition, she simply accepted it and declined to beat herself up over it.

Susan's need for autonomy was also evident in her nutrition choices. She did not like to be told what she could and could not eat, preferring to make her own decisions. We agreed that Susan would be allowed to eat whatever she felt like eating – as long as it was in line with the purpose of achieving her fitness goals.

Susan's Behavioral Strategy

By the end of her tour, Susan was feeling more in control of her wellness, and also her life and her job. Yes, she had also lost a few pounds – but perhaps more importantly, she had defused the rationalization that it was too hard to be healthy while on the road. Now she knew that it was possible to be healthy anywhere.

Susan was smart enough to know that her challenge would be to stay motivated after arriving home – to remain in the action stage, rather than slip back into contemplation or pre-contemplation.

With her newfound sense of mastery over her health and fitness, combined with an unstoppable enthusiasm, Susan returned to work more determined than ever to improve the workplace culture and help her employees to be healthier. Confident that it was the right thing to do, she began to take charge of introducing this concept, even without buy-in from Karen and Bill.

In the week she returned, Susan called a lunchtime meeting of all 80 employees and told them about her recent experience. She told her workforce that she had arranged with a local gym to offer any employee who wanted it a highly discounted corporate rate and 10 free training sessions to get started. She announced that three times a week, she herself would lead lunchtime walks in the immediate area of the business park where the headquarters were located.

She also promised that once every four weeks, a local health expert would come in to give a talk about some aspect of self-care, and that she was working on developing a companywide weight-loss fitness competition. She also asked for volunteers to help organize a healthy-lifestyle support group that could meet regularly and hold everyone accountable for their health behaviors.

She finished by saying that the company was offering a free health screening to help identify any health issues. These tests were voluntary and the results would of course be confidential.

Susan was earnest in her attempt to help her employees become healthier. She had experienced firsthand that being healthier makes us happier and more engaged and focused.

She also knew that changing her work culture into a healthy culture would reinforce her own efforts and keep her accountable – a key to maintenance. Now that she had made such a public display of her commitment, she could hardly fall back into her old habits.

Bill, the Chief Finance Officer, still wasn't convinced. He was still thinking only in dollars and wasn't sure there was much sense in Susan's initiatives. Karen, the HR Director, still wasn't terribly enthusiastic either. She continued to be fatalistic about her own chances of losing weight and becoming healthier, and focused on concern about potential extra work for her department.

Susan knew that both of her colleagues were stuck in their own change processes. She believed that Bill was stuck at first base, in pre-contemplation, not even seeing the need for any changes at all. She thought that Karen saw the need, but didn't think she could be successful – a common contemplation-stage holding pattern.

Susan forged ahead in spite of their doubts, but during one of our coaching sessions, she mentioned that she really wanted Bill and Karen to be on board and she was struggling with their lack of enthusiasm.

We discussed how Susan's strong sense of mastery could become focused on controlling uncontrollable elements, such as other people. I pointed out that rather than trying to change other people's behavior, the only thing we can truly control is the way *we respond* to their behavior.

We set up a context in which, instead of seeing her colleagues' behavior as a negative deterrent, she instead practiced seeing it as a positive challenge. We also spent some time together talking about the brain's resistance to change, and how the mirror neuron system could still be activated in Bill and Karen if Susan demonstrated her investment in her own health and led by example. This gave Susan the sense of proactivity and hope that she needed.

We also decided that I would come to help launch the company wide initiative by running a two-day Headstrong Performance program with her leadership team.

This hope and support enabled Susan to access her resourcefulness further. Instead of focusing on the naysayers in her company, she took time to identify people in her organization who would be enthusiastic and help spread the word. She realized she couldn't just wait for Bill or Karen to develop motivation or take ownership.

Jill, an administrator in Susan's office and a very sociable and health-conscious person, proved to be Susan's first advocate. Susan talked to Jill at length about her plan to change the corporate culture, and Jill got on board quickly, offering to create materials and devise an incentive program.

Susan gave Jill the autonomy to develop the initiative, and this newfound sense of liberty enabled Jill to come up with a powerful yet simple incentive idea: "You can leave 15 minutes early on every day that you participate in an aspect of the program."

Bill and Karen took part in the two-day Headstrong Performance program that I led, as did a number of other senior executives. During the program, Bill's excitement was captured by evidence of the potential return on investment offered by health initiatives. The game-changer for him was seeing hard numbers supporting not only a decrease in absenteeism but increased productivity.

During our program, I also introduced the leadership team to our integrated brain health assessment, the Headstrong Performance Assessment. For Karen, the turning point was a revelation that brain capacity and physical health are intricately linked. The possibility that her brain capacity was declining as she avoided taking charge of her health was incentive enough for her to consider participation in the wellness initiative.

After I left, Susan was still up against some resistance, but that didn't stop her from doing her best to inspire health in her co-workers. In the first week of the program, only three people showed up to walk with Susan, but that only made her want to try harder. She had learned to see challenges for what they are and she accepted them wholeheartedly. She even found herself inspired by the challenges. She knew she needed to lead by example, and that made her feel strong.

Soon, several other employees started taking advantage of their complimentary sessions at the gym, and an increased energy buzz in the office was palpable. Karen and Bill finally began to join Susan on her walks, and once they did so, many other employees began to join the walks and take part in the other initiatives as well.

Results

Within a few months, the program had caught fire. Joseph in the billing department had lost more than 20 pounds. Rachel, in marketing, had quit smoking and was at the gym several times a week. Throughout the company, people were making better choices in the lunchroom.

The support group was well-attended, and participants would often go out together afterwards and enjoy a healthy dinner. Later, Jill organized a weight-loss competition that almost everyone participated in. Each month Susan would recognize a staff member who had made significant health gains.

At their annual leadership meeting, Bill showed through his financial analysis that the culture of wellness had improved morale – and in turn, productivity. With the same workforce, the distribution team had managed to ramp up productivity, which re-established consumer trust in the company. Susan's sales team had improved sales, closing the cash flow gap from the Wal-Mart deal, which was also starting to gain momentum and was drastically improving revenue.

Karen disclosed that a cultural survey showed a substantial increase in employee engagement – and for the first time, employee turnover had dropped by a whopping 30 percent.

During one of our follow-up sessions, Susan shared how excited she was about the results. She'd had a strong instinct that it was a good idea, but never anticipated that a wellness initiative could yield such dramatic results for her, her employees and her company.

Susan learned that being healthy is not just a personal responsibility, it's an organizational responsibility with unimaginable emotional and financial gains.

Chapter Fifteen

Putting It All Together

"The three great essentials to achieve anything worthwhile are:
Hard work, Stick-to-itiveness, and Common sense."

Thomas Edison

One day about 10 years ago, I decided to break my bench press record.

For some reason, I'd had a mental block when trying to press beyond my maximum. Even though I could easily bench press 220 pounds, the moment I raised the weight by 5 pounds, I would fail miserably. I just could not do it. It felt like the 5-pound increment was 100 pounds of extra weight.

No matter how hard I tried to psych myself up, a voice always whispered inside my head that I was going to fail, that I would drop the weight on my chest and wouldn't be able to lift it off.

I *consciously* knew that I had the potential and strength to bench press 225 pounds. But the moment I would hear that familiar whisper, all the strength and confidence would leave my body. So I failed again and again.

What was going on? My conscious brain knew I was able to lift the weight. But my emotional brain feared that I would injure myself. That fear paralyzed me, hurtling me into a limiting sense of self-belief. I actually began to believe that I was *not* capable of lifting that weight off my chest, and over time simply gave up trying to improve beyond 220 pounds.

Breaking a personal fitness record may not seem like a big deal. But many of us struggle with this type of self-limiting dialogue in many aspects of our lives. For some of us, it may occur when we fail to lose weight or get healthier, or to secure that career-defining contract, or perhaps to finish writing that book that we've always wanted to write.

No matter what the arena is, I'm sure we've all experienced those voices in our heads. Unfortunately for many of us, those voices can be so powerful that we begin to *believe* we are incapable of achieving what we actually could, and simply stop trying.

Famed motivational coach Tony Robbins once said that limited self-belief leads to limited action, which then leads to limited results. Limited results only serve to reinforce a limited self-belief, thus forming a failure cycle.

But with positive self-belief, a success cycle can occur. If we can take the appropriate action that creates desired results, this in turn feeds into a greater self-belief. Our wins raise our potential to perform beyond our perceived limitations.

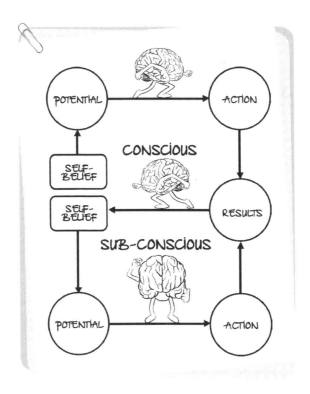

Research in neuroscience affirms this self-reinforcing cycle, which can either help us succeed or can prevent us from ever reaching our potential. What's tricky is that we not only have one cycle of thinking and belief occurring in our brains, but two. One cycle resides in our conscious brain, within our prefrontal cortex. The other cycle resides in our subconscious, emotional brain — and this one can greatly influence the conscious success cycle.

My bench-pressing endeavors offer a perfect example. My prefrontal cortex firmly believed that I had the potential to increase my personal best by 5 pounds, and as I positioned myself on the bench for the press, my conscious mind did everything right. It even tried to focus on positive messaging to "psych myself up."

However, the past experience of failure at this task was embedded in my long-term memory. This had a direct feed to my emotional center deep in my brain. And this part of my brain was more concerned about keeping me safe and preventing injury than it was interested in me achieving my personal best.

Therefore, just as I would lift the bar out of the rack and get ready to lower it to my chest, the subconscious success cycle would kick in and remind me — ever so subtly — that I was going to fail again. A message was sent to my conscious brain — my prefrontal cortex — that I simply did not have the strength. This message would override the conscious brain's knowledge, and result in yet another failed lift.

The failed result would then feed back into my limiting self-belief, which eventually resulted in me simply giving up.

Now, years later and armed with this new neuroscience knowledge, I decided to revisit this self-limiting dialogue during my bench press. I began to work on a strategy to see if it was possible for me to surpass my maximum bench press simply by changing the dialogue in my subconscious brain.

In exploring this dialogue, I discovered that my subconscious brain was feeling afraid that I might injure myself or drop the bar on my chest. These feelings were entering into my prefrontal cortex.

Hoping to mitigate the fear, I set out to make my emotional brain feel safer by asking a friend to be my spotter when pressing, just in case I actually wasn't able to make the lift. As I lowered the bar to my chest, my friend stood behind me ready to help if required.

I took a deep breath in and focused on how amazing I felt in the moment, and how grateful I was for having a spotter watching over me. As soon as the bar touched my chest, I gave every ounce of my being to raising it back to its starting position.

Oddly enough, the bar felt lighter than it had ever been. Without any assistance required from the spotter behind me, I managed to exceed my personal best. And by doing so, I proved to my subconscious brain that I *was* quite capable of doing this lift – and since then I've been able to repeat the feat. I managed to quiet that self-limiting voice.

My success, as small as it may seem, has significant ramifications for us all. Overcoming a limiting self-belief is not impossible – as long as we're prepared to "rewire" our cycle of thinking. We can do that by listening to and understanding those inner voices – and then finding a compromise, solution or reassurance that makes the subconscious brain feel safe.

Why am I telling you this story? Because after reading this book, if you're anything like me, you might be inclined to enthusiastically try every strategy contained within it during the very first week. And just as my subconscious brain was concerned for my safety and therefore limited my ability to succeed in my bench press, chances are your brain will be concerned for your safety too.

Of course by now, we've learned a lot from previous chapters about how to manage an overloaded brain, but if we overload the subconscious brain with too many new strategies in one go, it might become overwhelmed and inhibit our progress. A better strategy may be to take it one strategy at a time. The key, then, is to allow the brain to adjust to new routines and strategies, so it can feel empowered from its wins, rather than overwhelmed.

For that reason, I have created a development program that can help you progress and smoothly transition to these new ways of thinking, seeing and acting, so you can get the most out of your brain for years to come.

Periodization and Performance

Developed in the 1960s by coaches of Olympic athletes in the Soviet Union, *periodization* is the systematic planning of an athlete's training over an extended period of time – sometimes for years! Its purpose is to ensure that the athlete's adaptation to training is progressive, so they reach a level of peak performance at exactly the right time: the Olympic games.

Since the fall of the Soviet Union, the concept of periodization has become widely accepted by all of the world's leading authorities in athletic coaching. Two of the greatest challenges for coaches and athletes are the prevention of boredom and overtraining, both of which are detrimental to performance success. Periodization has proven to be one of the most effective methods of preventing boredom and overtraining.

Periodization divides an athlete's development into different phases, or cycles, that are devised to be just long enough to ensure maximum gains – but short enough to prevent boredom and overtraining.

A macrocycle, as it is called in periodization, is the athlete's entire training period. This can be anything from a few months (common when training for a particular race or competition) or it could be 4 years (in the case of Olympic athletes).

The macrocycle is divided into a series of subcycles called mesocycles and microcycles, each of which is followed by a transition (or rest phase).

As an example of what a periodized training model might look like, here is how I have developed periodization models for endurance athletes, many of whom not only improved their sports performance, but also ended up winning races. My athletes would spend the first few months building endurance. Once they achieved an acceptable level of endurance, I would transition them into a few months of building strength and power, which would help them build speed.

Finally, a few months prior to the race, I would transition my athletes into a phase of doing race-specific training to prepare optimally for their competition. After the race, I have the athlete take a few weeks off to fully recover from the race and training, which is known as the transition phase.

After working for years training athletes in sports performance, and training executives in mental performance, I have learned that both populations respond best when following a structured periodization plan. The only difference between athletes and executives would be that athletes follow a periodized training program to improve sports performance as where executives would follow one to improve mental performance.

Headstrong Performance Periodization Program

In Chapter 12, we examined behavior change and explored how emotion strongly influences the amount of time it takes to learn a new behavior. In a 2009 article published in the "European Journal of Social Psychology," researchers investigated how long it takes for the average person to form a new habit. Their research showed that it takes anywhere from two to eight months of daily practice for new behaviors to become a habit – whether it's drinking a bottle of water with dinner, or going for a 15-minute run before dinner.

With this in mind, we can extrapolate that it will take a minimum of two to eight months of daily practice to turn the strategies in this book into daily habits. As with athletes, following a similar periodization model will enable you to adapt gradually to new behaviors without feeling overwhelmed, but will also allow for enough variation to prevent boredom.

Your Headstrong Performance Periodization Program will be divided into two mesocycles (subphases) of three months. Each three-month mesocycle will be subdivided into three microcycles: the *resilience phase*, *sustained attention phase* and *creativity phase*.

Weeks 1 to 12

In the first week, complete just one exercise session of the routine outlined in Chapter 4, followed by two sessions in the second week, three in the third week and four in the fourth week. This is the resilience phase. As for nutrition, start with your hydration during your first week. The recommended amount of water intake per day should be between two to three liters per day, according to the Canadian Dietetics Association. During your second week, introduce a resilient breakfast, such as oatmeal. In your third week, try to have two meals per day with high-resilient foods. Finally, in week four, try to have all meals with high-resilient foods.

After you have completed your first four weeks, you will go on to another block of four weeks (microcycle two) – now practicing and mastering the sustained attention exercise and nutrition strategies from Chapter 7. Follow the same schedule outlined above to build up your sessions and nutrition, the way you did in the resilience phase.

Finalizing the first mesocycle in the creativity phase, practice and master the creativity exercise and nutrition strategies from Chapter 10. Again, follow the same periodization schedule outlined above in the resilience phase to build up your sessions over the first weeks.

As the number of exercise sessions and nutritional strategies increase each week, you may want to practice the PRIMAL model strategies from Chapter 13, which should help you stay on task and manage any challenges that come your way.

Once you have completed your first three-month mesocycle, you should feel confident and comfortable with the exercise and nutrition strategies in each of the microcycles.

MACRO CYCLE	MESO CYCLE	MICRO CYCLE		
24 WEEKS	WEEKS 13 TO 24	WEEK	24	: CREATIVITY
		WEEK	23	: ATTENTION
		WEEK	22	: RESILIENCE
		WEEK	21	: CREATIVITY
		WEEK	20	: ATTENTION
		WEEK	19	: RESILIENCE
		WEEK	18	: CREATIVITY
		WEEK	17	: ATTENTION
		WEEK	16	: RESILIENCE
		WEEK	15	: CREATIVITY
		WEEK	14	: ATTENTION
		WEEK	13	: RESILIENCE
	WEEKS 1 TO 12	WEEKS 9 TO 12 :		CREATIVITY
		WEEKS 5 TO 8 :		ATTENTION
		WEEKS 1 TO 4 :		RESILIENCE

Weeks 13 to 24

The second block (mesocycle) of 12 weeks works a little different from the first 12 weeks. By this time, your brain and body should be ready to handle more of a challenge. Instead of completing each phase over four weeks, you will only follow each phase (minicycle) for one week.

On Week 13, you'll do the four exercise sessions and nutrition strategies from the resilience phase that you completed in Week 4. In Week 14, you'll work on the strategies for the sustained attention phase as in Week 8. And on Week 15, you'll move on to the creativity phase as in Week 12.

On Week 16, you'll start over with these one-week cycles: one week each for the resilience phase, sustained attention phase and creativity phase. You'll continue these one-week cycles in order until you've completed all 24 weeks.

At the end of your 24-week periodization program, allow yourself two weeks of complete rest from physical exercise and any brain exercises. This is known as a transition phase. Those two weeks of rest are essential to allow the brain and body to recover from the past 24 weeks of training.

The one strategic aspect you don't need to "rest" from is nutrition – these new strategies should stay in place. As your energy demands increase through exercise, so might your energy requirements. Make sure to consume the appropriate amount of food to replenish energy by eating enough so you don't feel hungry (but not so much that you feel stuffed).

There may be days when your body and brain require more energy. If you feel this is occurring, simply increase your food intake by adding one or two healthy snacks, or increasing your portions moderately, choosing from the nutritious options suggested in the strategy chapters.

What to Expect

By following the schedule one week at a time, you'll become accustomed over time to the exercise program and to your new nutrition plan.

More importantly, you'll likely begin to notice some subtle changes week by week. After your first weeks following the resilience program, you will likely begin to feel stronger. Your energy levels will begin to improve as you become accustomed to your new nutrition program. Mentally, you may begin to feel more alert as the weeks progress.

During your second four-week block following the sustained attention program, the mental exercises might help improve your ability to maintain your attention for longer periods of time. Your nutrition program will enable you to continue to build mental vitality, which in turn will give you greater mental stamina. In your third block of four weeks, during the creativity phase, you will have the opportunity to enjoy the pleasures of play, which could put your brain into a state of relaxation, no matter how crazy the rest of your life might seem. This in turn will enable you to remain cool under pressure and exert a calming effect on those around you. You may also begin to enjoy periods of relaxed thought resulting in greater innovation and creativity.

Your second block of 12 weeks includes cycling between resilience, sustained attention and creativity on a weekly basis. Cycling this way may help strengthen that mental capacity you have been building. In turn, you may begin to notice a greater capacity to get more things done in a day, in less time. In other words, your performance capacity will likely increase as you progress through this program.

As you maintain your workouts and nutritional practices, you will very likely improve both physically and mentally. As you go through your mental and physical change, you may begin to inspire people around you. When this happens, share your experiences with them, and allow others to be moved to change too. Give them room to move through the stages of the Integrated Transtheoretical Model of Change.

If your experience is anything like mine and the experiences of my clients, you'll notice that this way of living leads to brain and body health, and cultivates positive leadership. This not only changes us for the better, but also changes the ones we care most about. We can begin to shape a new environment around us that echoes our newfound happiness, passion, performance and productivity in life and work.

Tools for Your Journey

*"No problem can be solved from the same level
of consciousness that created it."*
Albert Einstein

As you commence on your journey of improved performance, you will need access to resources to expand your consciousness about your health and performance.

The contents of this book are just the beginning. To help you along on the wonderful discovery of the body and the brain, you will need access to in-depth material and all the latest advances in the field.

I also know that people learn differently. This is why I have created a place where you can access the pioneering research, learn new techniques and applications and even get personalized coaching.

Get FREE resources
now at
HeadstrongPerformance.net

Assessments

Take 2 minutes and try my FREE Self-Assessment on my website for a quick overview on whether your lifestyle behaviors are priming you for superior performance. Want a more comprehensive assessment, including brain testing? Complete my proprietary Headstrong Performance Assessment. Complete it with your team and get a comprehensive, 22-page report full of useful information and suggestions.

Keynotes

Book me for a speaking engagement at one of your leadership conferences or events. These keynote addresses deliver a basic and experiential introduction to the numerous factors required for superior performance by executives. The presentation is ideal for a broader audience with minimal time investment, such as during corporate events and leadership retreats.

Workshops

Interested in learning how to improve performance through health and neuroscience? Sign up for one of my Headstrong Performance Workshops or book me for an exclusive Leadership Workshop in your organization.

Executive Coaching

For a more exclusive approach to attaining superior levels of performance, my Executive Coaching sessions involve priming the brain for superior performance through nutrition, exercise and neuroscience, followed by a goal-oriented executive coaching methodology to enable new insights and neural pathways. The empowering solutions can be found within you.

Webinars

Join me for a variety of online teaching events that focus on the science and application of Headstrong Performance.

Find out more about these resources at HeadstrongPerformance.net

Be a Headstrong Performer, Join the Community

Join Marcel Daane, and many thousands of Headstrong Performance enthusiasts. Our community is ever growing and we invite you to join us in our quest to be the best that we can be in all areas of life. Here, we share the latest news, ideas and research, and open up the forum for mindful discussion. Share with us your experiences and get answers to your questions from other Headstrong Performance enthusiasts around the world.

Our community members are committed to their performance and are always seeking ways to upgrade themselves to greater levels of health, thus priming their brains for superior performance capacity.

Blog and Email Newsletters

Sign up for the *Headstrong Performance Blog* on HeadstrongPerformance.net, and receive periodic emails that provide the latest news, research, applications and opinions. You will get lots of free ideas and tools for you and your entire organization.

LinkedIn.com/MarcelDaane

If you are an executive – and even if you are not – connect with Marcel through LinkedIn. Then join the Headstrong Performance group for more networking opportunities and great ideas.

Twitter.com/HeadstrPerform

Keep in touch wherever you are by following Marcel's twitter feed. Be the first to know what's going on in the world of Headstrong Performance.

Facebook.com/HeadstrongPerformanceBook

Be a fan of Headstrong Performance and like the page. Follow all the latest happenings from around the world and remain up to date on all offerings and workshops.

YouTube.com/ Headstrong Performance

The online video home of Headstrong Performance gives you access to dozens of videos on neuroscience, nutrition, exercise and performance.

About Headstrong Performance

Named after the book, Headstrong Performance is a Singapore-based, management consulting practice, focused on helping global organizations and individual clients to effect real improvement in mental performance, adaptability, resilience and leadership behavior by building a holistic foundation of health and fitness.

Once primed for superior performance, individual executives and leadership teams undergo intensive executive coaching to put their growing brain capacities to good use in business and in life.

Ranging from mental and physical assessments to customized executive coaching programs, we have the unique ability to not only build capacity in the brains of our clients, but also to help them develop the necessary skills to put their mental performance to good use.

Today's competitive economy is forcing organizations to make leaner talent management decisions by requiring a more agile and adaptable workforce that can effectively respond to, and take advantage of, market demands. What this means is that today, executives work more hours per week, with much more pressure than ever before, and this results in an increase in stress and exhaustion, leaving our executives susceptible to accelerated aging, burnout and even chronic disease. At Headstrong Performance, we aim to turn that equation on its head and cultivate talent that thrives under pressure.

Email / Web
info@headstrongperformance.net
HeadstrongPerformance.net

Meet Marcel Daane

Marcel Daane is one of the pioneers in integrating health and neuroscience to improve performance in executives. With over 20 years of coaching experience across business, sports, health and cognitive performance, his integrated approach has transformed the lives of thousands of executives and has subsequently helped improve the performance of numerous multi-national organizations from a wide variety of industries

Headstrong means determined, focused and committed and Marcel learned from the best about what that really means. His mother was exiled but ultimately honored by South Africa for her courageous stand against apartheid. Marcel's own life-journey has taken him from military service in naval intelligence, to coaching Olympic and professional athletes, and ultimately into executive and leadership coaching.

Marcel holds a postgraduate degree in the Neuroscience of Leadership from Middlesex University and an Undergraduate Degree in Complementary Medicine from Charles Sturt University coupled with advanced certifications in fitness and performance coaching.

About This Book

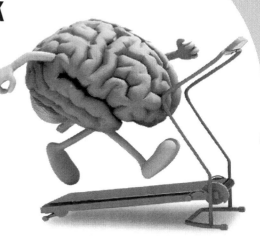

In today's dynamic business climate, despite technological advances, executives spend more time at work than ever before. Faster moving markets, shorter deadlines, constant change, and tighter budgets, all mean greater pressure and increased energy demands.

Headstrong Performance explores the research behind the deterioration of executive performance as a result of stress mismanagement and reveals the neuroscience behind stress and poor health behaviors commonly witnessed in the workplace and demonstrates how these coping strategies result in employee disengagement, decreased business performance, and subsequently a bottom-line that suffers.

Moving beyond the research, this book also provides a number of highly effective, health performance strategies that will enable today's professionals to remain on top of their game and work towards improved sustainable business performance for years to come.